THE TALES OF ISE

The TALES of ISE

translated from the classical Japanese

by H. JAY HARRIS

CHARLES E. TUTTLE COMPANY
Rutland, Vermont & Tokyo, Japan

Representatives

For Continental Europe:
BOXERBOOKS, INC., *Zurich*

For the British Isles:
PRENTICE-HALL INTERNATIONAL, INC., *London*

For Australasia:
PAUL FLESCH & CO., PTY. LTD., *Melbourne*

For Canada:
M. G. HURTIG, LTD., *Edmonton*

This translation is based on the Sanjōnishi Family manuscript in the collection of Gakushūin University, in photographic reproduction, edited by Dr. Suzuki Tomotarō and issued by the Musashino Shoin.

Published by the Charles E. Tuttle Company, Inc.
of Rutland, Vermont & Tokyo, Japan
with editorial offices at Suido 1-chome, 2-6, Bunkyo-ku, Tokyo

Library of Congress Catalog Card No. 70-167934
International Standard Book No. 0-8048-0745-0

First printing, 1972

4615 0293-000289
PRINTED IN JAPAN

TABLE OF CONTENTS

LIST OF ILLUSTRATIONS

ACKNOWLEDGMENTS

MY MOST sincere thanks are due to Dr. Tomo-ichi Sasabuchi, *professor of comparative literature at Tokyo Women's Christian College, who gave me an understanding of the depth of the original while he was a Fulbright exchange professor at Georgetown University, and to Dr. Kenneth Yasuda, associate professor of Japanese literature at Indiana University, who taught me translation as a demanding but fulfilling art. I must also acknowledge my gratitude to Professor Theodore Bowie and the Fine Arts Library of Indiana University for their permission to reproduce the illustrations of the 1608 edition of* Tales of Ise, *to Iwanami Shoten for permission to use materials in the appendix adapted from* Kōjien, *and to Sanseido for similar permission regarding material in* Meikai Kogo Jiten. *Thanks are also due my wife and family for their constant exercise of patience and understanding.*

FOREWORD

by Kenneth Yasuda

THERE HAS probably been no period in the history of literature in which a courtly society placed as much emphasis and importance on poetry as did the Heian period (794–1185), when lyric was a living part of everyday life. And few periods of which we know attained the sensitivity to elegance and to refined perceptions which permeates its literature. Scholars and literary historians have given us splendid intimations of this world, beginning with Arthur Waley's translation of its greatest work, the *Genji Monogatari* of Murasaki Shikibu (*ca.* 978–*ca.* 1016). This present version in English of *Ise Monogatari* by Jay Harris continues to enrich our understanding, for the *Ise* is a unique, aesthetic expression of the classic Japanese culture which produced the author of some of its poetry, who in his turn became an inspiration for later writers. Murasaki knew the work well. Fujiwara no Teika (1162–1241), the major poet of his day, seems to have lived with it, since there remain at least six copies of it in his hand.

[11]

Poets give us insights into our world. Great poets give us insights into human life. Arihara no Narihira (825–80), the author of the most memorable poems in the *Ise Monogatari,* is such a poet, one of the greatest of all the court poets. And he is even more, for he has become a name larger perhaps than life. His poetry has permeated Japanese sensibility, for the episodic structure of the *Ise Monogatari,* as elusive as the process of life itself, reveals with every episode, in its own illuminating way, the spirit of search and response in a man who loves love and the beauties of nature. Narihira, idealized in the figure of the "young man," is not only the hero of the tales but also the figure of a successful lover and the whole man, alive and responsive to the fabulously sensitive range of the Heian age.

The success of the present translation in part lies in its ability to convey through English constructions the experiential intent of the Japanese passages. And this, at times, without footnotes! The famous cherry-viewing scene (episode 82) is an example. The sense of the leisurely expansive and deliberate pace of the pleasures of a spring day among the cherry flowers seems to me to rise unmistakably as much from the spaces between the short sentences as from the sentences themselves. The masterfulness of the Japanese prose, which is admired for its understated simplicity and elegant freedom from mannerisms, is here not a quality we need to be told about but one that we can appreciate directly from Mr. Harris's rendering.

INTRODUCTION

The world speaks to me in pictures,
my soul answers in music.
—RABINDRANATH TAGORE

THESE WORDS of the Indian poet express the aesthetic truth which *Tales of Ise* has offered to Japanese literature for over a thousand years. Each of the 125 episodes, composed of sketchily drawn prose pictures and lyrically emotional poem-music, is a human truth, an embodiment of the Aristotelian *ethos*.

Tales of Ise stands as one of the two parents of a great body of romantic literature* produced during the tenth and early eleventh centuries. These romances, or *monogatari*, were the product of a society of aristocrats centered in the capital of Heian-kyō (the modern Kyoto), a city of some nine square miles with a population of several hundred thousand in the year 900. This was a society ruled to an amazing degree by a canon of aesthetic taste, and the most important of its ideals was labeled *miyabi*, or courtly elegance.

With this *monogatari*, as with all works of antiquity,

---

* The second is *Taketori-monogatari*, or *The Tale of the Old Bamboo Cutter*, which appeared probably during the first decade of the tenth century. *Taketori* represents that line in the *monogatari* tradition emphasizing the fantastic and supernatural.

it must be realized that conclusions will be more hypothetical than factual. Of the large number of *monogatari* mentioned in the contemporary and slightly later works of fiction, diaries, histories, and annals, fewer than a dozen are extant today in anything but fragmentary form. In the case of *Ise-monogatari*, scholars can do no more than speculate as to its authorship and date of composition. Any attempt to present these two questions for the general readership would necessarily become involved in the presentation of unwieldy amounts of textual and critical data. I do not propose to treat the various hypotheses advanced, but neither do I feel we can totally ignore the question. What I will offer is my own speculation in outline form.*

ARIHARA NO NARIHIRA

Approximately one-third of the poems in *Tales of Ise* are the work of the ninth-century poet Arihara no Narihira (825–80). This fact, combined with the similarity between many of the events in the present work and the poet's life, led many premodern scholars to suggest that Narihira was the author. This theory is untenable because the work includes materials and

---

* This speculation has been primarily influenced by the work done by Dr. Fukui Teisuke, collected in his work *Ise-monogatari Seisei-ron* [Theory on the Formation of *Ise-monogatari*], 1965. My own research, however, has led me to concentrate more on the aesthetic import of the whole *monogatari*, rather than on the process itself.

relates incidents which postdate 880. Nevertheless, we must look closely at Narihira the historical figure in order to understand the nameless, idealized central character of *Tales of Ise*. Particularly of interest in this respect are Narihira as he fulfills the ideal of *miyabi* and Narihira as a poet.

Arihara no Narihira was the fifth son of Prince Abo (792–842), a son of Emperor Heizei (r. 806–9), by a secondary wife, Princess Ito, a daughter of Emperor Kammu (r. 781–806). He held various official posts at the Court during his fifty-six years and at his death was concurrently the Temporary Governor *(in absentia)* of both Sagami and Mino provinces. The *True Annals of Three Reigns (Sandai Jitsuroku)*, a historical work written in Chinese which covers the years 858–87, describes Narihira as follows:

> In appearance elegant and comely,
> his self-indulgence notwithstanding,
> seriously wanting in Chinese learning,
> a fine craftsman of the native poetry.

This description is quite unique: it is most unusual for the official and semiofficial histories to comment on physical appearance, so we must assume that Narihira epitomized the ideal of physical beauty at that time. The second phrase seems to indicate that his social behavior was ruthlessly individualistic in spite of the strictly prescribed rules surrounding the aristocracy and the Imperial Court. The eighth and ninth centuries saw tremendous influence from T'ang China,

伊勢物語

and—while a native Japanese script had been devised for recording the language of the times—normal social intercourse as well as all official actions were recorded by the educated male elements of the aristocracy in either Chinese or Sino-Japanese. Thus, for Narihira to lack knowledge of the Chinese classics is most interesting, more particularly so in light of the last phrase of the description. In all the histories Narihira is the only poet mentioned as excelling in the composition of poetry in the Japanese language. Considering the stature of several poets of the earlier Nara period (710–84) who figure in the *Manyōshū* (759), the earliest anthology of Japanese poetry (and who are mentioned in the histories but not as poets), our attention is clearly to be focused on Narihira as a poet. Thus, in sum, Narihira appears to have been a dashing, individualistic courtier who was famed in his own time as a consummate master of the Japanese poetic form.

The importance of Narihira as a poet is further borne out by the fact that he is included among six poets who have long been designated the "Six Geniuses of Poetry" (*Rokkasen*).* These poets are singled out by the author of the preface to the first Imperially Ordered Collection, the *Kokinshū,* compiled in 905. Of Narihira the following comment is made by Ki no Tsurayuki:

As for Arihara no Narihira, his emotional

* In addition to Narihira they are: Bishop Henjō, the priest Kisen, Ōtomo no Kuronushi, Bunya no Yasuhide, and the poetess Ono no Komachi.

content proves too much for his techniques of expression; his poetry thus resembles the faded flower which has lost color while still retaining its fragrance.

The concepts of emotional content (*kokoro*, "heart" or "spirit") and concrete verbal expression (*kotoba*, "words") combine with the idea of poetic unity (*sugata*)—the total effect of the poem—to make the earliest formulation of Japanese poetics. For many centuries Tsurayuki's comments on Narihira were construed as a less than admiring criticism. It is probable that such was the intention, for Tsurayuki was determined to establish his own concept of poetic quality as a standard. This standard called for a more reasoned creativity, a poetic impulse more intellectual than that of the previous century.

Nevertheless, if we take a less predetermined critical attitude toward Narihira's poetry, we may view just those points which Tsurayuki considered faults as Narihira's assets. There is clearly no denial that Narihira is a master of the *uta* form. The *uta* consists of five lines totaling 31 syllables arranged 5–7–5–7–7. We need not view Narihira as a poet whose *kokoro* and *kotoba* do not harmonize in the unity of the *sugata*; we might rather say that his emotional content fills *and* overflows the form. The poetry of Arihara no Narihira thus transcends the *sugata*, harmonizing with the aesthetic ideal of the transient.

Two factual circumstances are the basis for my speculation on the process through which *Tales of Ise* developed. The first of these is that in volume 16 of the *Manyōshū* we find a large number of poems which are preceded by fictional or semifictional stories written in classical Chinese. These stories bear a striking resemblance to the narrative style found in *Tales of Ise*. A second phenomenon is that of the *kashū*, or private (individual) poetry collections. In addition to a Narihira *kashū*, there are numerous contemporary collections extant today. All of these *kashū* seem to be the poet's own "selected poems" kept in journal form, that is, with headnotes indicating the circumstances under which specific poems were composed.

We begin the speculative formulation by asserting that Narihira kept a poetic journal in which he recorded those of his poems which he felt best represented his art, along with their respective headnotes (*kotobagaki*). This journal, being a cumulative selection, will not have had any ascertainable thematic order.

At Narihira's death in 880, this journal will have passed into the collection of the immediate kinship group of the Arihara clan along with other such papers as the poet left behind. At this point I speculate that a relative (not necessarily a blood relative), aware of the existence of this journal, proposed to transform the substance of the Narihira *kashū* into a memorial to

Narihira as a cavalier poet.* The embodiment of this
aspect of Narihira is found in episode 69 of *Tales of Ise*
in which the hero achieves an illicit relationship with
the Shrine Priestess at the sacred Ise Shrine. There
exists a fragmentary text of *Ise-monogatari* known as
the *Koshikibu Naishi-bon* which is supposed to begin
with this episode. In support of my speculation that
this earliest version was intended as a tribute, there is
the fact that this same text reputedly concluded with
the following poem, found in episode 11 of the present
text:

> Do not forget me!
> As far distant as the clouds
> are we now: and yet,
> like the moon that rides the sky
> back again, will I meet you.

Though there is no evidence to either confirm or deny
my guess, I would hypothesize that this tribute version
was in existence by the beginning of the tenth century.

I would not, in any seriousness, attempt to attach a
name to the individual who produced my hypothesized
commemorative version. I would say, however, that
long experience with the original text has convinced
me that *Tales of Ise,* in each of its versions, must have
been written by a man—just as the *Tale of Genji (ca.*

* A more detailed discussion of this aspect, the cavalier nature,
may be found in the notes to episodes 25 and 63.

1008), the work which is the artistic culmination of the *monogatari* genre, is necessarily the product of a woman novelist.* In the note to episode 107 I suggest that Fujiwara no Toshiyuki (d. 907) could have been the author of this early version. He was Narihira's brother-in-law, which might have afforded him access to the original *kashū,* and a poet of substantial merit—being among a later selection of thirty-six master singers of the Nara and Heian periods (710–1185). This suggestion is made primarily to explain the nature of the characterization of Toshiyuki the historical figure. While it is impossible to eliminate him from the list of possible authors, his name has only minor relevance to my general speculation on the development of *Ise-monogatari.* I have mentioned Toshiyuki here solely to indicate the kind of man who would have been the author of the tribute version.

Sometime between the compilation of the *Kokinshū* (905) and the *Gosenshū* (951), another of the Imperial collections, *Tales of Ise* assumed its present form (excepting, of course, interpolations made by later copyists.)** During these years, the ideal of *miyabi,* courtly elegance, held reign over the aristocratic society of the capital city. Someone—and in this case it would be

---

* Literary history identifies her as Lady Murasaki Shikibu, but details of content and expression would indicate the author's sex were this work, too, of uncertain authorship.

** These interpolations generally provide links between the story line and Narihira's biography; this biography, however, was influenced in retrospect by *Tales of Ise* because the readership thought of the hero and Narihira as often being equal.

futile to guess at a name—reconceived the potential in the tribute version of *Tales of Ise*. He will, I hypothesize, have clearly recognized the vital emotional character of Narihira in the nameless hero. Being himself ruled by the spirit of *miyabi*, the author of the now standard version will have set himself the task of recreating the earlier version so that the new product would relate the life of a still nameless hero who, idealized and redefined in symbolic mold, would embody that social aesthetic ideal. In so doing, this author devised a carefully random sequence of 123 episodes, each—as stated at the beginning—a human, aesthetic truth. At the head of this sequence he placed the episode which relates the events following upon the hero's coming of age; this initiation, in terms of the social ideal which is the essence of the whole work, is equivalent to birth. Finally, at the end of the sequence he placed the "death poem," producing the 125 episodes translated in this volume.

LYRIC AND NARRATIVE: A DIALOGUE OF FORM

For the most part, it is still natural to view most of Western literature in terms of the formal concepts set forth by Aristotle in the *Poetics*. Only during this century have we seen the development of fictional forms which successfully break away from the governing principle of plot. Again, it is primarily during this century that Japanese fiction has made use of a deliberately structured plot, in the Western sense, as the basic technique of the novel.

Tales of Ise, as suggested above, manifests a purposively conceived randomness of progression, but we cannot identify any plot for the whole. The *Tale of Genji,* a work perhaps twenty times as long as *Tales of Ise,* has been discussed in terms of its plot by both Western and Japanese scholars, but this seems to me merely an attempt to facilitate conclusions about the novel genre in world literature. After forty volumes dealing with the life of the Shining Prince, from his birth through middle age, we would expect to find an account of his death. This is omitted, however, and the novel goes on for another fourteen volumes. *Genji-monogatari,* rather than having a unified plot in Western terms, seems to be formally controlled by the novelist's concepts of the transient world, the aesthetic society, and, most importantly, causality. The actual formal structure of *Genji* is the episode, and this concept of form is first realized in *Tales of Ise.*

The episode as a formal structure may derive from the poetic journals (*kashū*) or the "story-poems" in volume 16 of the *Manyōshū;* or there may be a more primitive and universal urge to storytelling behind both of these.* The unique contribution of *Tales of Ise* is the dialogue of formal elements achieved in its structure by the interrelation of lyric and narrative qualities.

Poetry—or, more properly, song—has always held

---

* This seems to be evident in the quasi-historical *Kojiki* (712), which combines prehistory, history, and cosmogonic myth in annal form.

precedence among the literary forms in Japan. It has never been removed from the pattern of daily life to be placed upon an almost unreachable pedestal. For this reason, it is difficult to discover in the earlier period a dichotomy between poetic and prosaic diction. Poetry—for the Heian society the *uta* in particular—remains an emotionally charged extension of prosaic speech. The narrative sections of *Tales of Ise* seem almost to be afterthoughts which have been displaced and put before the *uta*. The narrative quality of the prose style, terse and often ambiguous, seems definitely dependent on the lyric nature of the poetry. This relationship creates a structural tension as a binding force which arises from the episodic quality (*tampensei*) of the whole. While the episodic structure of the *Tale of Genji* appears much more extensive, it is proportional to the broad scope of the work: the unity and completeness of the individual episode (or volume) remain inviolable.

HEIAN JAPAN

The society depicted in *Tales of Ise* should not be equated with that so scrupulously detailed in the *Tale of Genji*.* Rather, this earlier period saw several clans

* The most readable descriptions of this society may be found, if not within *Genji* itself, in the study by Dr. Morris cited in the Bibliography, chapters 10–12 of George Sansom's *Japan: A Short Cultural History*, and chapters 6–9 and 11 of Sansom's *A History of Japan to 1334*.

still in contention for the dominant position in the political system. There are a number of episodes in *Tales of Ise* which deal with the political eclipse of the Ki and Arihara clans. The complete victory of the Fujiwara family, whose clan chieftains served as chiefs of state for the powerless emperors, was not yet an accomplished fact. Similarly, the aristocracy of the ninth century,* while clearly isolated from the major portion of the population,** had not yet begun to descend to the condition of stagnancy which augured the end of an epoch.

The nebulous conglomeration of Buddhism and Shinto which, along with imported systems of astrology, geomancy, and supernatural superstitions, governed the everyday life of the characters in *Genji* may have been present, but these influences were minimal. While documents from this period do little to enhance our knowledge of Japanese society during the ninth century, there are three relationships which must be understood in order to appreciate *Tales of Ise*. These are the relationships between man and nature, man and Court society, and man and woman.

* This is the century depicted in the work as indicated by episodes 1 and 2, though we have set the composition of the tales in the tenth century. Similarly, *Genji-monogatari* depicts tenth-century Heian society.

** The aristocracy, those who received rank and title from the Court, probably numbered five or six thousand; estimates of the total population of Japan for the period range from one to four million.

The eighth century, which produced most of the *Manyōshū* poets, was an age in which the pioneer spirit (*masurao*) established the clear (*sei*) and bright (*mei*) as ruling aesthetic ideals. The still-young Japanese nation established its capital at Nara, a city modeled on Ch'ang-an—seat of the T'ang government in China—and adapted much of the imported culture to the needs of a country still at war with the less "civilized" Ainu tribes at its borders. The Imperial House was firmly established as the ruling line, but the league of aristocratic clans still carried the task of securing the continued existence of the state. This era of emphatic virility was one in which man maintained a daily direct communion with nature.

The ninth century must be regarded as a transitional period. The potential and reality of a native Japanese civilization distinct from that of China was gradually entering the national consciousness. Continuity of the state had been secured, and the Court and aristocracy had settled into the often austere but aesthetically satisfying life of the new capital at Heian-kyō. It was an age for reflection. While the Capital was unquestionably the center of aristocratic life, the outlying districts and provinces had not yet—as in the tenth century—come to be viewed as the wilds of exile, areas in which man no longer existed as a social being. The individual had not yet found it necessary to confine himself within the walls of his estate, fashioned in what is known as the *shinden-zukuri* style of architecture.* This style was already current in the ninth century, but in addition to his formal garden the aristocrat of these times could still accept the aesthetic reality of beauty in its natural setting; and he could still, when necessary, deal directly with it.

As suggested above, the aristocratic society was severely small in number. It consisted of the Imperial Household with its blood-related families and the major and minor clans—which seem to have developed from a differentiation of functions: worship, war, manufacture, etc.; these were organized into patri-archal hereditary families.** Within the confines of this select group, almost every detail of the conduct of daily life was prescribed according to rank. These pre-scriptions ranged from manner of speech, dress, degrees of luxury and ostentation to the opportunities for education, political advancement, and social mobility. This system was in operation during the ninth century, but as seen through *Tales of Ise* it appears much less resistant to occasional violation than in the tenth-

---

* Estates of this type were surrounded by thatched walls. Inside these were a formal garden with artificial mountain and lake, various small bridges, garden pavilions, a carriage house, servants' residences, and the main complex of buildings situated at the back. The latter included a central building occupied by the head of the estate, a building to the north (behind the central structure) reserved for the formal wife and her entourage, and buildings to the east and west for lesser wives and concubines with their attendants. All these buildings were connected by means of open galleries.

** There is much evidence to indicate that this patriarchal organization was preceded by a clearly matriarchal system. Many of the legendary and early rulers were empresses.

century society of the *Tale of Genji*. Again, this seems to be a transitional stage between the earlier pioneer spirit and the foreboding of stagnation.

The relationship between man and woman during the early Heian period is simultaneously the most important and most difficult aspect of *Tales of Ise*. The specifics of relations between the sexes as presented in the work are unclear at best, while the later Heian literature is biased from the other side, having been written by women. Nevertheless, several helpful generalizations can be made. Despite their lack of social mobility in a consciously patriarchal hierarchy, the women of Heian Japan were the main owners of property and thus important actors—indirectly—in the political structure. Consequently, the more fortunate women of the aristocracy were much sought after by men wishing to enhance their futures. Moreover, in a polygamous society which was in a period of transition, the possibilities for romance and intrigue were virtually limitless.

The reader will quickly discover that to a great extent *Tales of Ise* is a catalogue of the hero's romantic affairs. It is naturally tempting to compare this man with a Don Juan type, but the comparison will not prove true in any of the many characterizations of Don Juan. On the whole, Don Juan was a failure both as a lover and as a man; his approach to life destroyed rather than created him. This is wholly untrue of the hero of *Tales of Ise;* he is somehow enriched by each of his amorous adventures. This enrichment is not—as in *Genji*—dependent upon the success or failure of the relationship; nor does it matter whether the woman is a future empress (as intimated in episodes 4–6 and randomly throughout) or an uncultured lady in the provinces (as in episode 14). The world depicted in *Tales of Ise* is one in which romantic alliances are the central material. This fact indicates the cavalier nature of the idealized hero and, to speak of content, shows the manifest filling-and-overflowing of emotionalism so characteristic of Narihara's life. The manner of expression, analogously the "words," is so designed as to temper the content with *miyabi* to produce a unity of the two which is the ultimate achievement of this masterpiece of Japanese literature.

LITERATURE IN TRANSLATION

I have attempted in this translation to reproduce not only the substance but also what I conceive to be the intent of the original. I cannot claim that this is either patently achieved or wholly possible as there is no perfect translation. But I suggest that *Tales of Ise* must first and most importantly emerge as a work of literature. To this end the reader should be aware of my method of translation and the way in which this work is presented.

In translating both the prose and poetry of *Ise-monogatari,* I have avoided wherever possible all use of archaic diction. Though the original is archaic (or classical) Japanese, and though it would have been possible to utilize equally obsolete English diction, I have followed the principle that the readership must determine the mode of expression. In translating the prose, I have adopted an often unusual system of punctuation in order to give the reader some sense of the rhythm and flow of the original.

The translations of the 209 *uta* in *Ise-monogatari* were achieved with the following principles. I have maintained the 5–7–5–7–7 syllabification of the original in all cases. Whenever possible the sophisticated word plays, associative meanings, stock epithets, and other poetic conventions and devices (such as the acrostic in the first poem of episode 9) have been retained or transferred into equivalent devices. Most importantly, I have labored to make Japanese *uta* into English poems.

In order to present *Tales of Ise* as a work of literature, all notes have been arranged together after the text. These notes include explanations of the cultural, literary, and historical material relevant to each episode. Further, I have occasionally pointed out in these notes specific problems of translation which may be of interest to the general reader. No attempt has been made to incorporate discussions of lexical or grammatical problems in their scholarly detail, as this has been well done by Dr. Vos in his two-volume study.* While the notes and this introduction are intended to assist the reader in a fuller appreciation of the work, I have tried to concentrate my efforts on making the translation a romance independent of them, complete in and of itself.

* See Bibliography.

THE ILLUSTRATIONS

The woodblock illustrations reproduced in this book are the work of an unknown artist of the Tosa school. They originally illustrated the first printed edition of *Ise-monogatari*. This was produced by the calligrapher and publisher Suminokura Soan (personal name: Yoichi; 1571–1632) in the thirteenth year of the Keichō era, 1608.

The 1608 edition is in two volumes, 27 by 19 cm. (10½″ by 7½″): 51 sheets in the first volume (25 prints) and 64 sheets in the second (24 prints). This edition is one of the earliest illustrated printed books produced; Soan's residence in Saga on the outskirts of Kyoto gave this type of book the genre name *Saga-bon*. Since this edition uses variously colored pages, it is also known as *goshiki-bon* (five-color edition). The text was printed with movable type, and the calligraphy is believed to be that of Soan himself.

Suminokura Soan studied calligraphy under the great calligrapher-artist-esthete Hon'ami Kōetsu, but later developed his own distinctive style and school. As a great lover of the Japanese classics, he was—together with Kōetsu—one of the first to employ movable type in the mass production of printed books. In producing this edition of *Tales of Ise,* Soan had his text verified by the court noble and scholar Nakanoin Michikatsu (pen name: Yasokusō; 1558–1610) who wrote an afterword to the edition.

The copy of this 1608 edition used here is in the collection of the Fine Arts Library of Indiana University. There were six printings of the 1608 edition; this copy is not from the first printing as it lacks the written seal (*kakihan*) of Michikatsu, but it seems to be from the second or third since later printings have an additional afterword by Soan.

The Tosa school of painting maintained the "pure" Japanese tradition as opposed to the Chinese style used by artists influenced by Sung landscape painting and portraiture. Theirs was the style which traced back to the Heian Yamato-e style of the picture scrolls. There is an emphasis on line and the well-known perspective gained by removing the roof of a building to show the interior. During the Muromachi period the Tosa school was influenced to a certain extent by the Chinese style; in these prints that influence is evident in the brushwork used for rocks and trees. Nevertheless, these prints are not greatly different in style from those paintings of *Ise-monogatari* which might have been made for the Picture Contest described in the seventeenth chapter of the *Tale of Genji*.

伊勢物語

THE TALES OF ISE

✤ DAN I

Long ago, a young man came of age and, having an estate in the village of Kasuga near the old capital of Nara, went hawking. There lived in that village two very elegant sisters. This young man contrived to peep at them through the fence. Finding such beauty so unexpectedly in the dismal decline of the old city, he was captivated by them. Cutting the cuff from the hunting cloak he was wearing, the young man wrote a poem and sent them in. The young man had on a hunting cloak of the mottled purple Shinobu pattern.

> Fields of Kasuga
> with whose tender purple shoots
> this gown has been dyed:
> This confusion of my heart
> whose boundaries no man knows . . .

Thus like a man beyond his years did he compose and send his song.

*　　*　　*

1. *"This young man contrived to peep at them through the fence."* (Dan I)

And would he not have gradually thought more
wonderful things—

> From Michinoku
> come the patterns of hateweed:
> Who may be the cause
> of emotions muddling—
> I am not the source of this.

Such was his meaning. The men of former times thus
felt such deep elegance.

✦ DAN II

Long ago there lived a young man. When the capital
at Nara had been left behind and the houses of the new
capital were not yet in order, there lived a woman in
the Western City. She far outshone the common
women. Indeed, her nature even surpassed her outward
beauty. It seems she did not lead a single life. This
earnest young man became intimate with her and
returning from his tryst probably wondered how
things were. It was the first day of the third month,
and since the rain was gently falling he sent this poem:

> Without arising
> nor slumbering—this last night
> I met dawn with you:
> Today, as a part of spring,
> I while away like the rains.

✦ DAN III

Long ago there lived a young man. Thinking to send around some duckweed to the place where the woman he loved was staying, he wrote:

> If you love me still
> even in some shabby hut
> would I lie with thee:
> Our bedding no rich duck's down
> on spread out sleeves we'd settle.

*　　*　　*

This event occurred when the Consort of the Second Ward had not begun her service to the Emperor and was yet a commoner.

✦ DAN IV

Long ago when the Empress Dowager was residing in the Eastern Fifth Ward there was someone living in the western wing of her palace. The young man, though at first thinking her too unattainable, now set his heart upon meeting with her and went to pay a call, but though it was only around the tenth of the first month she had secluded herself elsewhere. Though he had heard where she was, it was not a place a common man might visit, and he felt increasingly pained and could do nothing. In the first month of the

2. "Sad at heart, he lay on the mean wooden floor until the moon set . . ." (Dan IV)

following year when the plum trees were in full flower he returned to this western wing wistfully thinking of the previous year. Though he tried standing and sitting as he looked about, there was nothing resembling the past. Sad at heart, he lay on the mean wooden floor until the moon set, and with the memory of the year past he recited:

> The moon: is it not . . .
> the spring: is it not . . . last year's
> spring yet unchanged? No,
> this body of mine alone
> seems the same as once before.

Thus with the dawn faintly breaking he returned in tears.

✦ DAN V

Long ago there lived a young man. Very secretly he went to the vicinity of the Eastern Fifth Ward. Because his visits were to be unknown he could not enter from the gate, so he would slip through a break which the servant children had made in the earthen wall. Though there were few who knew of his visits, the master of the house caught wind of it since these trips were so frequent. He had a guard posted at this "lover's gate" so though the young man might come he would return having been unable to meet his love. Thereupon the young man recited:

> At this unknown road—
> my gate through the earthen wall—
> Barrier keeper!
> Every day at evenfall
> may I wish you soundest sleep.

Reading this the girl became extremely out of sorts. Thus the master remitted and allowed his visits.

* * *

Because he visited the Consort of the Second Ward secretly and this was being talked of at Court, it was indeed her brothers who had the guard stand watch.

✦ DAN VI

Long ago there lived a young man. While for several years he sought the hand of a girl he could never make his own, in the end he stole her away in the black of night. When they reached the edge of the river called Akutagawa, the girl asked the young man "What is that?", seeing the dewdrops on the grass. They had come a long way and the night was falling fast. Because the rains were coming furiously and the thunder was terrifying, the young man squeezed the girl into a

3. *"He stole her away in the black of night."* (Dan VI)

shabby storehouse unaware that there were demons in the area. He stood outside, his bow and quiver readied. While he stood there wishing again and again that the dawn would come soon, a demon had already eaten the girl in one gulp. She had cried out in fright, but he could not hear her in the crashing of the thunder. As the night gradually gave way to the dawn, the young man looked inside. But the girl he had brought was gone. He stamped his feet in grief and wept, but it was no use.

> Can these things be pearls
> or what other could they be?
> When she asked me this
> no, they're dewdrops, I replied—
> Far better I had vanished!

*　　*　　*

Although this took place when the Consort of the Second Ward had presented herself for service at her cousin, the Empress's, the young man stole her and carried her off because the superb beauty of her countenance had so struck him. Her brothers—the Horikawa Minister and the Councilor of State, Kunitsune, the oldest—were then still without such high rank. Just at that time they were on duty in the palace and overheard someone crying terribly. They caught the young man and took back their sister. This was the so-called demon. The affair occurred while the girl was still quite young and without a high position.

✦ *DAN VII*

Long ago there lived a young man. When he left for
the Eastern Provinces finding it hard to enjoy life in the
Capital, he saw the waves rising in great whitecaps as
he reached the border between Ise and Owari. Here he
recited:

> Still more violently—
> For the one now left behind
> lovingly I yearn
> but see in mounting envy—
> The returning waves!

✦ *DAN VIII*

Long ago there lived a young man. He set out for the
Eastern Provinces saying the Capital life was unbearable. Seeking more livable surroundings, he went with
one or two friends. On seeing the smoke rising from
the peak of Mt. Asama in the Province of Shinano:

> Here in Shinano—
> From the peak of Asama
> white smoke billowing,
> near and distant travelers:
> Could anyone suspect them?

伊
勢
物
語

Long ago there lived a young man. His heart was full
of bitterness and, saying he could no longer live in the
Capital, he went off to the Eastern Provinces to make
a new home. With one or two of his old friends he
left. Because they were unfamiliar with the roads, they
went on rather bewildered. They came to a place called
Eight-Bridges in the Province of Mikawa. The reason
the place was so named is that the streams that joined
there formed a spider web, and thus eight bridges had
been set up. At the edge of a marsh in the shade of the
trees they dismounted and sat down to eat their dried
rice. In the marsh, some flags were blooming elegantly.
Seeing this one of them said, "Using the five letters of
'flags,' make an acrostic poem about the spirit of
travel." So the young man recited:

> Foreign raiments mine
> Lackluster by this time now
> As wife and master
> Gone so long along this road:
> Such is the heart of travel.

Hearing this, the others wept, and their tears fell on the
dried rice causing it to swell.

Continuing on, they reached the Province of Suruga.
At Mt. Utsu the road they thought to enter was quite
dark and narrow, grown over with ivy and maples.
Their minds were wandering aimlessly in such uneasy

4. *"At the edge of a marsh in the shade of the trees they dismounted . . ."* (Dan IX)

surroundings when they met a traveling ascetic priest. "What are you doing in such a place as this?" the young man asked. Looking closer, he saw he knew this priest. He wrote a letter to the one he had left behind in the Capital and gave it to the priest with this poem:

> Here in Suruga
> even near Reality Slope:
> No, not face to face
> no, nor in my dreams—my love
> I have no chance of meeting.

At the sight of Mt. Fuji where the stark white snow had fallen even at the close of the fifth month:

> Which knows no season
> this mountain is Mt. Fuji:
> What time should I feel
> seeing it thus fawn-spotted
> where the snow has deigned to fall?

If we compare this mountain to those of the Capital, it is probably almost twenty times higher than Mt. Hiei, and its shape is like that of a salt pile.

As they traveled still farther, there was a large river between the provinces of Musashi and Shimotsufusa. That is the river called Sumida. They stood together on the bank of that river, and their thoughts drifted: How terribly far we have come! And as they wept with each other, the ferryman said, "Hustle on to the boat now. The sun's already down." They stepped in, and the

[47]

boat pushed off. But everyone was lost in sad thoughts of their ladies at the Capital. Just then they saw a white bird with red beak and feet, about the size of a snipe, eating fish while scudding on the surface. Since this bird was unknown in the Capital no one knew what it was. When they asked the ferryman, he answered, "Why, that's a capital gull!" Hearing this the young man recited:

> You shoulder such a name—
> Well, I've a favor to ask—
> Oh, Capital Gull!
> Is the lady whom I love
> yet at home unharmed or no?

Without exception, everyone in the boat fell to weeping.

✦ DAN X

Long ago a young man wandered as far as Musashi Province. There he courted a certain lady. Her father said he was going to marry her to someone else, but her mother was determined the girl have a nobleman. The father was a commoner, the mother a Fujiwara. Thus it was that she thought only of the nobility. To this prospective son-in-law she sent this poem she had recited. She was living in the village of Miyoshino in the Iruma District.

[48]

From Miyoshino
the wild goose on the rice fields
in all earnestness
to that place where you are now
draws near with suppliant voice.

The intended bridegroom answered:

To where I am now
that nears with suppliant voice
from Miyoshino
the wild goose of the rice field:
Could ever I forget her?

Not even in the provinces did he forsake such diversions!

Long ago, while traveling through the Eastern Provinces, a young man recited this poem and sent it back to some friends:

Do not forget me!
As far distant as the clouds
are we now: and yet,
like the moon that rides the sky
back again, will I meet you.

✦ DAN XII

Long ago there lived a young man. He stole away someone's daughter and took her with him to Musashi Province. Even there, however, because he was a kidnapper he was captured by the provincial governor. Before this he had hidden the girl in the tall grasses and made his escape. Some men who were coming along the road said, "They say this is the field where that kidnapper is . . ." and they were about to set fire to it when the girl, beside herself, recited:

> Field of Musashi—
> Do not burn it down today!
> Like the young grasses
> here my lover crouching hides
> and I too lie in hiding.

Hearing this, they captured her as well and led her off with the one who had already been taken.

✦ DAN XIII

Long ago, a young man who was in the Province of Musashi wrote to a woman in the Capital—"Should I mention it to you, I'd feel embarrassed; yet saying nothing also is unkind . . ." On the letter-wrapper he wrote "Musashi Stirrups" and sent it off. Because there was nothing after this, the woman in the Capital recited:

5. *"They were about to set fire to it . . ."* (Dan XII)

Stirrups of Musashi:
Though I know you've tossed me off
still for news I yearn—
To query you is painful,
to query not vexatious.

Seeing she had written thus, the young man felt it to be unbearable and recited:

Vexed if I tell you,
begrudging it if I don't!
Stirrups of Musashi:
Hanging on Dilemma's horns,
why not this life surrender?

✦ *DAN XIV*

Long ago, a young man traveling aimlessly came to the Province of Michi. A woman of the area, thinking probably that a man from the Capital was more than extraordinary, earnestly became infatuated with him. Consequently she recited:

On the contrary!
While I do not die of love . . .
as a silkworm, yes,
better far to have been born
in spite of its short-lived life.

Even her poem was countrified! Nevertheless, the young man took pity on her and went and slept. Because he left while it was still night, the woman recited:

> If it had been dawn . . .
> I'd drown him in the washtub
> dirty old rooster!
> Cockadoodling when he did
> has driven my man away.

The young man said, "I go back to the Capital," and recited:

> Were you as upright
> as the Pines of Areha
> at Kurihara—
> A knick-knack for the Capital
> would I take you back with me!"

She was delighted and said to herself, "Why, yes, he seems to care for me!"

✦ DAN XV

Long ago in the Province of Michi a young man called on the wife of a commoner, and thinking her to be far too fine for her husband he recited:

Over Mt. Desire
I would go but secretly—
For such paths I long
that to the deepest valleys
of your heart I might hasten.

The woman thought to herself how wonderful it
would be to have such a lover, but then "how should
I show a heart as refined as his one like mine which is
so rude and countrified . . . !"

✤ DAN XVI

Long ago there lived a man by the name of Ki no
Aritsune. He had served three Emperors and had been
at times quite influential; but then the men and the
times changed. He became no more—perhaps even
less—than a common man. He was a man of a beautiful
heart, loving things elegant and refined, in no wise like
the ordinary man. Now even though his days were
spent in poverty his heart and spirit were as they had
always been, as though the hard realities were not
present to him. The wife with whom he had shared life
so long at long last left their marriage bed to become
a nun, as her sister had before her. Though theirs had
been no great love, her husband was deeply saddened
at the thought of her going now. But he was penniless
and could not even afford the usual gifts of parting.

Overwrought, he wrote to a friend of long standing: "... and so, she is leaving now, and I cannot even make the least offering ..." And at the bottom he added the poem:

> On these hands of mine
> the years we spent together
> one by one I count:
> While my fingers count to ten
> they count it four times over.

The friend, seeing this, was overcome with the sadness of the situation and sent a full wardrobe from cloaks to night clothing, and along with it this poem:

> Even though the years
> are ten four times repeated
> that your match has passed,
> countless times has not your wife
> come to trust and count on you?

Receiving such gifts and sympathy, Aritsune recited:

> Can it truly be ...
> Heaven's fabled Feather Robes
> these appear indeed!
> True enough, for you, my Lord,
> have made of them your present.

Still overwhelmed, he added:

Has the autumn come?
Is this dew that wets my sleeve—
So it seems at least:
Else it is just that my tears
have fallen all unnoticed.

◆ *DAN XVII*

Not having paid a visit for too long a time, a man came
flower viewing at the height of the cherries. The owner
then recited:

Fragile and short lived:
Such is the reputation
of the cherries' flower—
Only rarely in the year
he comes, and they await him.

The reply:

Were it not today
I'd come, tomorrow like snow
they'd swiftly fall:
Or else still on these branches
would they blossom as before?

✦ DAN XVIII

Long ago there lived a rather inexperienced girl. A young man lived nearby. The girl, knowing he was a great lover of poetry and thinking to get a look into his heart, plucked a fading chrysanthemum and sent it to the man's residence with the poem:

> So faintly crimson
> is it tinged: where sleeps this hue?
> Much like the white snow
> fallen to cover the branch
> and its true color it seems.

The young man, pretending not to catch her meaning recited:

> So faintly crimson
> are its petal's edges tinged—
> White chrysanthemum:
> Much like the crimson-lined sleeve
> of her who plucked it it seems.

✦ DAN XIX

Long ago a young man had an affair with one of the ladies-in-waiting of a woman who served at the Court. Before long, his ardor cooled. Since they were in the

6. "*The girl . . . plucked a fading chrysanthemum . . .*"
(*Dan XVIII*)

same house the woman saw him often, but for his part the young man acted as if she were invisible. The woman recited:

> Like the drifting clouds
> distant, far removed from me
> you have now become!
> Nonetheless, before my eyes
> visions of you come wafting. . . .

In reply to this the young man answered:

> Like the drifting clouds
> to a distance now removed
> for this long time past:
> On that peak which once was mine
> the gales are blowing strongly.

Besides, it was said she had other lovers.

❖ DAN XX

Long ago a young man saw a woman in the Province of Yamato. He was attracted to her and made himself her lover. So it was, and after a while he had to return as he was in the service of the Court. On the way back the young man broke off a spray of maple that was delightfully colored like the autumn maples though it was only the third month. From along the road he sent it back to the woman with this poem:

> Only for your sake
> this spray which I have gathered
> while it is still spring
> behold! so like the autumn,
> with all its colors aflame.

The woman's reply was brought to him after he had already reached the Capital.

> Without my knowing
> this sudden change in color
> seems to have occurred:
> Perhaps in your home village
> it really is spring no more?

✦ DAN XXI

Long ago a young man and woman shared a very great love, caring for none but each other. So it was, and yet . . . might there not have been something, something small she noticed? The woman thought her lover was tired of her and thought to leave him. She recited this poem and left it attached to a screen:

> If I go away
> "Woman of the fickle heart"
> will not all men say?

> But of our relationship
> they know not the half, and thus . . .

Such was her parting note as she left. That this woman had gone leaving such a note the young man found strange as he could remember nothing he had done to cause it. What could it have been? He wept most bitterly and wondering where he should seek her went out through the gate. He looked everywhere but could find no trace of the way she had taken, so the young man returned to the house.

> No use for loving
> such a world it has become:
> All these months and years
> with only unmeaning vows
> have I truly been living?

Thus he recited and fell into sullen reveries . . .

> Oh, how does she now . . .
> is she still thinking of me?
> Like a jeweled hairpin
> a vision of her alone
> pierces my sight more and more.

The woman had been away for a long time when, perhaps no longer able to bear up, she sent the poem:

> Now no more perhaps—
> But the grass of forgetting

or even one seed
into your heart's deep furrows
I had no desire to sow.

His reply:

This forgetting grass
if you would know where it grows
look to your own fields:
"In these fields only love grows"
how I long to believe it!

Then, much more than in the past they exchanged
letters and poems. The young man:

Perhaps forgotten—
The heart admits this thought in
learning how to doubt:
Much more than ever before
it is something most forlorn.

Her reply:

On the horizon
the clouds rise up and are gone
leaving not a trace:
My life but a vacant dream
in the winds of your mistrust.

Such feelings they exchanged. But each had taken his
own way in the world, and thus they had grown too
far apart.

[62]

伊
勢
物
語

Long ago there were a man and a woman who had broken off their relationship over a trivial matter, but —perhaps she had still not forgotten him—there came from the woman:

> Bitter, nonetheless—
> Yes, this man who once was mine
> I cannot forget—
> All the while I'm hating him
> likewise I am loving him!

And because such was her poem, the man said, "Just as I supposed!" and recited:

> With our former love
> let us be now of one heart
> like river waters
> separate as they skirt the isle
> to flow on joined forever!

Thus he sang and went to her that night. They spoke together of the past and their future and other sundry things. The man recited:

> The long autumn night—
> Multiply one thousand times
> count this now as one—
> Should we lie eight thousand nights
> together, would this suffice?

She replied:

> The long autumn night—
> Multiplied one thousand times
> made as one—and yet
> things to say remain unsaid
> as the cock crows in the dawn . . . ?

More so than in the past the man held her dear and continued his visits.

✦ *DAN XXIII*

Long ago the children of some country traveling peddlers had played together at the well, but since they had grown up they were shy and embarrassed with each other. Nevertheless the young man thought to make the girl his wife, and the girl wanted this boy for her husband. Though their parents tried to arrange other matches, they would have none of it. Then there came from this young man next door the poem:

> By the barrel-well's
> built up crib I'd pull myself
> measuring my height:
> I've shot up like a willow
> this long while we've been apart.

The girl sent back:

7. *"The children . . . had played together at the well . . ."*
   (Dan XXIII)

> Since we vied for height
> my once childish hair has grown
> beyond my shoulders:
> If it is not to be you,
> who then best should tie it up?

They continued to exchange such love notes and finally were married as they had desired.

Well, as some years passed the woman lost her parents, and their life as husband and wife became rather hard. "Is there no escape from this impoverished life I lead . . ." thought the man, and consequently he took a mistress in the Takayasu District of Kōchi Province. So things stood, but when his proper wife showed no signs of reproving him and even sent him off to this mistress, the man thought she, too, had probably taken up with someone else. Full of this mistrust he hid himself in the garden thicket as though he had gone to Kōchi. From there he saw his wife beautifully made up straing out into the distance.

> As the wind blows up
> off shore the whitecaps mounting
> Mountain Dragon Scent:
> Does my Lord at the midnight
> cross there all alone and safe?

Hearing her recite such a poem the man became immeasurably enamored of his wife and stopped going to Kōchi.

When on a rare occasion the man went to Takayasu

he saw the woman who at first had made herself so elegant now grown careless about her appearance. She took the rice ladle in her own hand and stuck it into the vessel. He became thoroughly disgusted and went no more to Takayasu. His mistress thus sat looking out toward Yamato and recited:

> Toward your native home
> staring listlessly I live:
> Ikoma Mountain,
> do not hide yourself in clouds
> even if the rains should fall!

She lived thus listlessly until at last the man from Yamato sent word that he was coming. Overjoyed she awaited him, but night after night passed, and she sent the poem:

> You would come to call,
> you said, but every evening
> I have lain alone—
> Though I no more sit and wait
> my days are spent in hoping . . .

But the man had quit with her for good.

◆ *DAN XXIV*

Long ago a young man lived with a woman in a

slightly provincial area. The man was in service to the Court and found parting to be most difficult, but did eventually go. He was gone for three years without even one visit, and the woman became sick of waiting. But on the very night she had promised to take an admirer of long standing as her new husband this young man returned. "Open the door, please," said he, but she would not. Instead she composed a poem and shoved it out to him.

> Like a lump of jade
> unpolished for three long years
> I waited darkly:
> Only on this night, indeed
> when I am pillowed elsewhere . . . !

He then recited:

> Like the warrior's bow
> of varied woods straight and true
> you stood time's trials:
> Just as we served each other
> serve your new Lord lovingly.

And when he started to go, the woman came back with the poem:

> This warrior's longbow
> whether it is drawn or not:
> More than in the past

                    unto you my Lord my heart
                    is drawn and would draw nearer.

But he was not to be stopped.
   The woman was utterly heartbroken. She followed
after him trying to catch up, but was unable to do so.
Coming to a place where the water ran silent and clear
she lay down, and cutting her finger on a craggy rock
that was there she wrote in blood:

                    With no pledge of love
                    drew my Lord away—yet I
                    could not make him halt:
                    Now indeed my life itself
                    has surely become unstrung!

There she died.

◆ *DAN XXV*

Long ago there lived a young man. He composed this
poem and sent it around to a woman who was being
overly coy with him, not having said she wouldn't
receive him . . . but.

                    In an autumn field
                    through bamboo grass at morning
                    sleeves trailed in retreat—

> From a night devoid of you
> how much more are they wetted!

This woman who knew all about such amours sent back:

> Clothed in murky weeds
> did I not appear to you
> an unwelcome cove—
> Fisherman with empty hands,
> homeward bound with dragging feet?

✤ DAN XXVI

Long ago a young man wrote in answering a friend who had been lamenting his lack of success with a woman in the Fifth Ward:

> Like a sudden storm—
> One's sleeve is like a harbor
> pounded by fierce waves
> as a great foreign vessel
> lumbers in to take refuge.

✤ DAN XXVII

Long ago a young man went to a woman's quarters

for one night and after that did not favor her again. 伊
Thus the woman pushed aside the bamboo screen over 勢
the basin where she washed her hands and looked at 物
her reflection in the water. She was all alone as she 語
recited:

> I and I alone—
> Those who sometimes think of me
> number only one:
> So I thought when there within
> the water was one other.

But the man who had come only once overheard her
and replied:

> In that same water
> might you not see me as well?
> Even the green frog
> at the bottom of the pond
> does not croak alone!

✦ DAN XXVIII

Long ago because a woman who was flirtatious picked
up and left:

> Why should it be thus?
> Now the vessel of our love
> seems to be a sieve—

So it would be watertight
we sealed it once, however . . .

❖ *DAN XXIX*

Long ago when his presence had been requested at the
Flower Celebration of a certain personage at the
palace of the Heir Apparent's mother:

Not quite in full bloom
have my sighs and sorrows been
always, until now:
But today at evenfall
their petals splendidly burst!

❖ *DAN XXX*

Long ago a young man wrote to the house of a woman
he had almost never visited:

This affair of ours
seems to be so foreshortened
as closely strung pearls:
Still that bitter heart of yours
tells its ever taller tale.

✦ DAN XXXI

Long ago at the Court, while passing in front of some
ladies' apartments and being taunted by someone bearing him some kind of hatred with the lines

> . . . I foresee this blade of grass
> anon shall wither away.

a young man countered:

> Should you call down harm
> on a man quite free of crime
> the forgetting grass
> will sprout upon your body—
> It says so in tradition!

But there were some ladies who thought this malicious.

✦ DAN XXXII

Long ago, to a woman he had once promised many
years earlier:

> As once in the past
> like the damask warp and woof
> we were closely spun:

Oh if only I could change
that past into the present!

Such was his poem, but it seems she hadn't a thought
for him.

✦ DAN XXXIII

Long ago a young man had a woman in the Mubara
District of Tsu Province he visited. Because she seemed
to be thinking that when he went away this time he
would never come again, the young man recited:

From among the reeds
swelling deeply comes the tide
ever, on and on:
So to you this heart of mine
flows with love ever fuller.

The woman returned with:

In a deep dark cove
drifts this brimming heart of yours:
By what ways or means
ought I then know its cargo
save you pole it out to me?

For a country woman's poem is this one good or bad?

✤ *DAN XXXIV*

Long ago a young man, to the residence of someone
who had been cold toward him:

> I'd speak but cannot,
> yet silence is but a ruse
> to my troubled breast:
> Only in my chambered soul
> can I dare to tell my wound!

Certainly this was an audacious manner of speech.

✤ *DAN XXXV*

Long ago, to the residence of someone he had broken
off with though such was not his real intention:

> Like a silken string
> twined into a hollow cord
> bound in harmony—
> Even though we've come apart
> once again would I meet you.

✤ *DAN XXXVI*

Long ago, to the residence of a woman who had put

the question to him "Should it not seem to me you
have completely forgotten my existence?":

> Narrow though the gorge
> even to the summit point
> the vine reaches up:
> That we should be torn apart
> has not once entered my mind.

✦ DAN XXXVII

Long ago a young man had an affair with a woman
who was well experienced in love. Was he not perhaps
a bit uneasy?

> If it is not me
> take care not to loose your sash!
> Oh, morning-glory,
> even though you are a flower
> that falls before the evening.

In reply:

> By the two of us
> was this sash tied at parting—
> One of us alone
> will not I think unloose it
> till we two are face to face.

[76]

❖ DAN XXXVIII

Long ago, having gone to Ki no Aritsune's estate and
finding that he had gone out walking and would not
return until late, the young man sent out the poem:

> It was due to you
> that I came to understand:
> In this world of men
> would not someone take my debt
> to be one paid back as love?

Aritsune returned:

> As I have not learned
> like the others one and all
> what or when or who,
> just what does this word "love" mean
> is a question I must put.

❖ DAN XXXIX

Long ago there lived an emperor who was called the
Emperor of the Western Palace. This emperor had a
child known as Princess Takaiko. She was taken from
this life, and on the night of her interment a young
man living next door who wished to view the ceremonies climbed into a carriage of court ladies as they
went off to find a good spot. The actual funeral proces-

sion itself did not begin for a long while, and while these ladies spent all their time weeping and mourning a man named Minamoto no Itaru, the handiest roué in the whole country, came over to their carriage. He too wanted to watch the procession and, judging theirs to be no more than a group of ladies, came over and was flirting and talking with them. This Itaru caught some fireflies and put them inside the ladies' screened carriage. But the ladies within were afraid perhaps the fireflies' light might expose them to critical eyes and greatly wished it might be extinguished. On that the young man who was with them in the carriage recited:

> Would the hearse draw by
> the last flicker of her life
> borne unto the wind—
> Lived she her full time? Ah, no!
> Hear the voices lamenting . . .

The poem this Itaru returned with was:

> With what great remorse
> all lament I am aware:
> Yet before the wind
> was this lamplight snuffed out short—
> It is far beyond belief!

For the poem of the handiest roué in the whole country this was rather disappointing!

*   *   *

Itaru was the grandfather of Shitagau. His bad behavior was not intended to show disrespect to the late
Princess.

✦ DAN XL

Long ago a very young and inexperienced man had the
misfortune to fall in love with a girl who wasn't really
too bad. His parents thought they knew what was best
in such matters and decided to have this girl removed
from their service and placed elsewhere. Such was the
decision they announced, but they had not taken actual
steps. Since this young man was totally dependent on
his parents' support, he had no power to oppose them
and could not stop her being sent away. What is more,
as the girl was only a mean servant, it was impossible
for her to object. In the meantime though, his feelings
grew stronger and stronger. Without any warning the
parents suddenly sent the girl away. The young man
shed tears of blood, but there was nothing he could do
to stop it. She had already been packed off in someone's care. Weeping, the young man recited:

> If this girl is gone
> who then now from taking leave
> could hold himself back?
> More than ever in the past
> do I bear such great sorrow!

And thereupon he stopped breathing. His parents were in a flurry. They had only tried to do the best thing . . . and, certainly, it couldn't be that serious! But as he really was no longer conscious they began to worry and had services and austerities performed in his behalf. At the hour of the dog* on the day after he had entered the coma just at sunset, at last the young man came alive again. Long ago young men had such violent passions. But I wonder if even today's old men would die of love!

✦ DAN XLI

Long ago there lived two sisters. One married a poor and common man while the other had a husband of high birth. The sister who was married to the commoner was washing her husband's Court cloak at the end of the twelfth month and shaping it with her own hands. Though she was trying to do her best, she tore the shoulder of the cloak because she was unused to such mean labors. She was at a loss for what she should do and thus fell to weeping and weeping. The man who was high born heard of this and felt it was really too unfortunate. Thus, he picked out a truly magnificent green cloak of the sixth rank and had it taken over with the poem:

* 7:00–9:00 P.M.

It is like the hues
deeply purple all alike
to the finest eyes:
So the verdure of this field
falls not to categories!

*　　*　　*

This must be the spirit of Musashi.

✦ DAN XLII

Long ago a young man exchanged words with a
woman even though he knew she was flirtatious.
Nevertheless, he thought no ill of her for it. Though
he went to her often, he was uneasy about her fidelity
—yet this did not quite stop him from continuing his
visits. At a point in their affair there were two or three
days when the young man was occupied with business
matters and could not visit and he wrote thus:

After I have gone
even footprints leading off
should remain unchanged—
For whom now are these perhaps
faithless stepping stones become?

This was written out of suspicion.

✦ *DAN XLIII*

Long ago there was an Imperial Prince named Prince
Kaya. This prince bestowed his love upon a woman
and was extremely solicitous toward her. But this
woman had a very elegant gentleman courting her.
Yet a third young man who thought she was his alone
heard of these others and sent her a letter. With a
picture of a cuckoo, the poem:

> Oh, gentle cuckoo!
> Since the hamlets where you sing
> seem so numberless—
> Yet have you flown far away
> who are my love's melody.

This woman, her feelings hurt, recited:

> Bird of many nests
> is what you now say of me
> as today I weep:
> When my wings would grow heavy
> I am denied all shelter!

It was just the fifth month. The young man replied:

> With so many nests
> fly then, gentle cuckoo, on
> only to alight
> in the hamlet where I dwell—
> May your welcome song not cease!

◆ *DAN XLIV*

Long ago he decided to have the farewell rites for someone who was going to take up a provincial post. Calling him to his own house, since this was not just a passing acquaintance, the young man had his wife set out the wine cups, and he made a present of a woman's garment. This young man who was the head of the house composed this poem having the waist cord of this trailing skirt tied to it:

> As you start away
> so for you, my friend, have I
> taken this skirt off—
> Though it and I both pass on
> may our friendship ever last!

*   *   *

This poem, of all those read, goes straight to our hearts in its depth of feeling and thus was not read aloud. How deeply impressive . . . !

◆ *DAN XLV*

Long ago there lived a young man. Someone's daughter who had been reared with the greatest care thought somehow to become intimate with him. Perhaps because she found it too difficult to speak her feelings, she fell ill. When it seemed she was dying this girl

8. *"The fireflies flew high into the sky."* (Dan XLV)

said, ". . . thus, indeed, would I have loved . . ." Her parents heard of this and weeping uncontrollably had it reported to the young man. Though he came with most solicitous concern and anxiety she died. There in her house he confined himself in mourning and deep thought. It was at the end of the sixth month when the weather was very hot—at night he would join in the music of the liturgy. As the night deepened a chill breeze gradually came up. The fireflies flew high into the sky. Watching them as he lay back this young man recited:

> Rising fireflies,
> even above the cloud peaks
> you must fly this night—
> I'd have you tell the wild goose
> where the chill fall breezes blow!

> One day of summer
> from dawning to setting sun
> long I sit and stare:
> With nothing left from the past
> all is but melancholy!

✦ DAN XLVI

Long ago a young man had a very good friend. They wanted never to be separated even for the shortest time, and when it happened that this friend was to go to the provinces they parted with the greatest of regret. In a letter to the young man sent after some time:

> ". . . How astonishingly long it has been since I have seen you! I wonder somehow if I have not passed from your thoughts and am pained . . . In this human existence it would seem friends ought not to be forgotten even though they are far apart . . ."

Since he had so written, the young man recited and sent this poem:

> Though we do not meet
> never entertain the thought
> you are forgotten!
> Times too numerous to count
> visions of you come to me!

✦ DAN XLVII

Long ago a young man somehow was entranced by a woman and thought to make her his. So it was, but she had heard that this young man was the lover of many women and her coolness toward him further increased as she recited:

> When so many hands
> try to take you as their own

answer to a prayer
even though I love you too
your fidelity I doubt!

In reply, the young man:

> Rumor has spread wide
> that I answer any call:
> Yet when cast afloat
> as I always am at last
> I wind up stuck in shallows!

✦ DAN XLVIII

Long ago there lived a young man. He was to lead the
rites of farewell and was waiting for the traveler to
show up. When he hadn't come:

> What a time to learn
> of the torture waiting brings!
> I myself am due
> at a different meeting place
> where I shall surely be missed . . .

✦ DAN XLIX

Long ago a young man used to regard his younger half-
sister with great interest. For her, he recited:

With your heart so young
I would lie down beside you
gentle, tender grass:
Yet how my heart is rended
to find you already plucked!

Replied she:

Not one single hint
ever passed my way that you
loved this young green grass—
May I hope you stay to see
other seasons in this field.

✦ DAN L

Long ago there lived a young man. Returning the
scorn of someone who hated him:

Even if you could
make a hundred fragile eggs
stack up one by one
should I give my love to her
who never would be faithful?

Because of this she recited:

As the morning dew
dries up except for one drop

[88]

9. "*More ephemeral | even than writing numbers | on a running stream . . .*"   (Dan L)

it is not all bad:
You are even more fatal
you deserve no trust at all.

Again the young man:

Maybe it could be
that last year's cherry blossoms
weren't blown off the bough—
Even then it's hard to trust
a person of your nature!

And the woman:

More ephemeral
even than writing numbers
on a running stream
would it be to love someone
who thinks only of himself!

He, again:

Like the running stream
and the age we now have passed
like the fallen bloom:
Who would counsel that we wait
for anything—who would hear?

*　　*　　*

This is a story of a man and woman who while seeing
who was more fickle were secretly going about in the
world hiding this nature.

✤ DAN LI

Long ago a young man, on having planted a chrysanthemum in someone's front garden:

> This chrysanthemum
> even without the autumn
> would it not still bloom?
> Though these flowers may wither
> yet its deepest roots live on.

✤ DAN LII

Long ago there lived a young man. In return for
having received a gay festival delicacy from someone:

> Just to cut sweet flags
> you have wandered high and low
> throughout the marshland—
> I have gone into the field
> to reap this prize of the hunt!

He sent this along with a pheasant.

✤ DAN LIII

Long ago a young man met with a woman who was

not easy to get in touch with. Because the cock crowed while they were still talking:

> How should it happen
> that the cock now signals dawn
> while the night is young?
> I have much yet to express
> ere my love and dawn are told.

✢ DAN LIV

Long ago a young man to a woman who had shown indifference to him, the poem:

> All my roads are barred
> save I trust the paths dreams take—
> As I lie alone
> do not the dews of heaven
> shed themselves upon my sleeve?

✢ DAN LV

Long ago a young man, in a world where it seemed he could never have a woman he had fallen in love with:

> Though it may be true
> that you never think of me

every time I hear
phrases you once have spoken
I sense a glimmer of hope!

✦ DAN LVI

Long ago a young man thought of love in sleeping,
thought of love in waking, never ceased to think of
love:

> Though my silken sleeve
> is no rough hewn hermitage
> hidden in tall grass
> as each day begins to close
> tears of dew seek its lodging.

✦ DAN LVII

Long ago a young man occupied his mind with a love
known only to himself. To the quarters of someone
who was indifferent to him:

> Like the measuring worm
> said to live in the seaweed
> reaped by fishermen—
> You have cracked my soul in half
> and now my love destroys me!

✦ *DAN LVIII*

Long ago a young man who was a ladies' man to the limits of his resourcefulness built a house in the place called Nagaoka and went to live there. Some ladies— who were not at all bad looking—who were with some ladies of the Imperial family next to this young man's house saw him as he tried to harvest the rice field and said, "What work for someone known to be such a famous lover!" When all together they came over and then into his house this young man escaped to the inner part of the house. As he hid himself away, these women sang out:

> Uninhabited—
> How many generations
> hid in random weeds?
> Its evanescent owner
> never pays a social call . . .

Because they had been so bold as to enter and then make such noise, the young man:

> Goose grass grows about
> making this hut stark wildness
> with a lonesome cast:
> Every so often demons
> gather here their shrieking horde!

This he sent out to them. When the ladies said, "Let's go glean the harvest!"—the poem:

Filled with boredom full
you would glean the fallen grains—
If I had but known
I would join your fair party
and venture out to the fields.

✤ DAN LIX

Long ago a young man—perhaps tired of the Capital—
decided to go live on Mt. Higashi:

No more can I live—
Now the point of no return:
In some mountain home
must I hide myself away,
now begins the quest!

In this state he became terribly sick, and when it seemed
that he was almost dead someone splashed his face with
water. As he began to breathe again he recited:

Over my body
a blanket of dew is spread:
Has it dropped from oars
of boats crossing the threshold
to heaven's starry river?

And thus he had come back to life.

✦ *DAN LX*

Long ago there lived a young man. When it came about that he was busy with affairs of the Court and he no longer truly loved her, his wife took up with another man who said he would love her with his entire being and with him went off to the provinces. The young man heard she was the wife of the Receiving Officer of a certain province while he was on an Imperial mission to the Usa Shrine. To this man he said, "Have the mistress of the house serve the wine cups or else I shall not partake myself!" Thus as his former wife offered the wine the young man took a wild orange that was in among the side dishes and recited:

> When I catch the scent
> of the wild orange blossom
> come in this fifth month
> how it calls back the fragrance
> of the sleeve my love once wore!

Hearing this she remembered the past with shame, became a nun, entered the mountains and remained!

✦ *DAN LXI*

Long ago a young man—when he had traveled as far as Tsukushi—heard someone say from behind a bamboo screen, "This is the one supposed to be such a great man with the ladies!"

> Certain it is fact
> any man who goes across
> River of the Dye
> will find his reputation
> colored with its lusty hue!

The woman replied:

> With no grain of salt
> must we take its very name
> Island of Deceit:
> Truly you wear a garment
> drenched in its peppery waves!

✦ DAN LXII

Long ago a woman who had been left alone for a long time—was she not perhaps dull—fell prey to a man who was not to be trusted. When she was in a gentleman's service in the provinces she came out and at the banquet waited upon the man who had been her former lover. When the evening came on, this young man said to his host, "Bring me that girl who was here earlier," and she was sent in. Saying to her, "Is it possible you do not recognize me?" the young man recited:

> Where that luster now
> in the past so beauteous?
> Flowering cherry
> only the bare trunk remains
> stripped of its flowers and branches.

But she was overcome with shame and sat there without answering. When he said, "You have not answered me . . ." she managed "With my tears brimming over I can neither see with my eyes nor find words to speak."

> Can it really be—
> Though you fled to escape me
> you have spent your stay
> in this same Meeting Province—
> Have you not yet grown wiser?

So recited her lover, and he removed his cloak and made her take it. But she discarded it and fled. Where she had gone he could not know.

◈ DAN LXIII

Long ago a woman who was fond of the ways of love wished very much to meet a man somehow who would lavish his affections on her. Though she thought this way, by no means could she make it known; so she made up a false dream. She called her three sons in and told them of this dream. The older two gave curt answers and left the room, but the third son interpreted it saying, "A wonderful man will come along!" At this the woman's mood brightened immensely.

This youngest son thought to himself—most other men have no feelings at all . . . I wish somehow I could bring her together with Colonel Zaigo! He happened to meet this officer when the colonel was out hunting. The son took the bridle of Colonel Zaigo's horse as he walked along the road and said, ". . . so that's how she feels. . . ." Hearing this Zaigo took pity on her and went and slept with her.

Well, afterwards when he didn't come again the woman went over to this young man's house and watched him through the fence. But the Colonel caught a glimpse of her and recited:

> Short by but a year
> of a centenarian's age
> with her wizened head—
> So seems the one who loves me
> a phantom before my eyes.

The woman saw he was about to leave and quickly returned to her own home, catching herself on the brambles and quince on the way, and lay down in her room. Just as she had done, this young man stood secretly outside looking in. Then the woman sighed deeply, said "I'm going to sleep," and recited:

10. *"The woman went over to this young man's house and watched him through the fence."* (Dan LXIII)

> On my narrow mat
> of bamboo I spread my gown:
> All this night as well
> must I sleep without meeting
> that person so dear to me?

The man thought how sad this was and that night went to her bed. In the ordinary, the way of love is such that if one loves one cares, if one loves not one takes no heed. But this young man was of a nature which made no such distinctions whether he loved the woman or not.

✦ DAN LXIV

Long ago a young man, incredulous as to where she might be from, recited to a woman who was not sharing his intimacies even in the privacy of letters the poem:

> Could I make myself
> like the wind that gently blows
> at your bamboo blind—
> Through its loosely woven chinks
> might I enter unto you.

In reply:

> Though there be a wind
> which I cannot hold in check

at my bamboo blind—
Who has deigned to give it leave
that it should seek my chamber?

✦ DAN LXV

Long ago there lived a woman who was loved by the
Emperor and permitted to don the forbidden vermilion. She was cousin to the lady who was then the
Empress Dowager. A young man of the Arihara clan
who served in the Imperial Audience Chamber was
extremely young, but he was quite intimate with this
woman. Because he was still permitted to go amongst
the ladies, when he would come to their dais in the
Great Hall and sit with her this woman said, "This is
horrible! I shall be ruined—come no more!" Said he:

> Should our deep felt love
> be so quickly overcome
> by merest caution?
> No, let us go on meeting
> with no fear of consequence!

And when she withdrew to her own chamber he
followed after, regardless of the others looking on. So
mortified was this woman that she returned from the
Palace to her own home. Thereupon, thinking what a
good opportunity this would be, the young man

went there to visit her, and when everyone heard of his shameless ardor they scoffed at him. The next morning he was seen by the Imperial Groundskeepers as he removed his riding boots, tossed them to the corner of his room and entered the Audience Chamber. To go on behaving so atrociously would surely lead to his utter destruction and dismissal; so this young man prayed to the Buddha and the gods: "What ought I best to do? Would that Thou remove my lustful spirit!" But he only became more ardent in his love, and when his infatuation had passed the point of reason he summoned diviners and Shinto liturgists. They went then to prepare the ceremonies which would exorcise this passion. Yet the more intently they purified the more impassioned the young man became, reciting:

> So my heart would cool
> was this sacred office made
> in Libation Stream—
> Yet it seems the gods disdain
> to hearken to my calling.

This said, he returned to his rooms.

The Emperor was a man with handsome features; the spirit of the Buddha deeply ingrained in him he chanted the Saving Name in a most reverent and harmonious voice. Hearing him this woman thought as she wept bitterly: What sins of a former life must I bear to be unable to serve such an August Majesty ...

and how unfortunate that I am shackled to this
Arihara. . . . And she wept. When eventually the
Emperor heard of the entire matter he banished the
young man, and the woman's cousin—the Empress
Dowager—had her retired from the Court and shut
away in a storehouse. Imprisoned in this cell she cried
as she was chastised:

> Like the measuring worm
> who lives within the seaweed
> reaped by fishermen—
> I drown in a sea of blame
> but never regret having loved!

From the province of his exile this young man came
every night and played exquisitely upon the flute and
sang in a voice of haunting sadness. Thus from within
her storehouse prison the woman heard him and
thought: Ah, it is my lover! But they could no more
meet face to face.

> Is he not aware
> that the love he bears for me
> cannot but be sad?
> Whether or not he meets me
> I am myself no longer.

Such was the poem that she heard within herself. The
young man, unable to meet her, went back and forth
in his exile and sang the poem:

Fruitless though it be
I am driven back and forth
for one thing alone:
That once more I might see her
I ride the wings of impulse.

*　　*　　*

This would have been during the reign of Mizu-no-O. The Empress Dowager was the Lady of the Damask Hall, also called Lady of the Fifth Ward.

✦ DAN LXVI

Long ago a young man, having some land holdings in the province of Tsu, set out for Naniwa taking along two brothers who were his friends. When they saw a stretch of beach and several boats, he recited:

Port of Naniwa
seen this morning for the first—
In each sheltered cove
ships that brave the seas are they
or passports to life's calm waters?

Everyone was deeply moved by this, and they headed back.

✤ *DAN LXVII*

Long ago a young man, in order to raise his spirits, invited a few people of the same mind and went to Izumi Province about the second month. As they looked out at Ikoma Mountain in the province of Kōchi the clouds were constantly shifting—first scudding over, then clearing. The sky clouded over in the morning and broke at noon. On the trees the branches were tipped with stark white snow. The young man was the only one among them who, seeing this, recited:

> Yesterday, today
> yawning clouds hide the mountain
> usually clear:
> Snow flowers leaf the forest
> making me cold and bitter.

✤ *DAN LXVIII*

Long ago a young man went to Izumi Province. As they went through Sumiyoshi Strand in the hamlet of Sumiyoshi in Sumiyoshi District the scenery was so enchanting that they dismounted and walked along with the horses. Someone said, "Recite a poem about Sumiyoshi Strand."

> More than crying geese,
> more than asters flowering

in rich red autumn—
Beauteous shoreline in spring
here at Sumiyoshi Strand.

Such was the young man's poem that none of the others was able to compose a line!

✤ DAN LXIX

Long ago there lived a young man. When this young man had gone to Ise Province as an Imperial Falconer, the mother of the girl then serving as the Virgin Priestess of the Ise Shrine informed her daughter: "You are to take greater pains with this person than with any ordinary emissary." Because it was her mother's wish she entertained him with the greatest courtesy. In the morning she assisted in the preparations for the hunt, and when he returned in the evening she had rooms for him readied in her own palace. Such was the care she took. On the night of his second day in Ise the young man said to her, "Let us meet by all means!" The girl herself by no means had any aversion to such a rendezvous, but as there were too many prying eyes it seemed impossible. Since this young man was the head falconer his rooms were at no great distance. Indeed, they were close to her own quarters; so the Priestess, making sure that everyone was sleeping soundly, came to the young man's rooms at the first watch of the hour of the rat.*

* 11:00–11:30 P.M.

11. *"He discerned someone standing in the hall with a little handmaiden before her."* *(Dan LXIX)*

He himself had been unable to sleep and lay staring out into the night when in the faintness of the moon's light he discerned someone standing in the hall with a little handmaiden before her. Overjoyed, the young man let them into his sleeping quarters. She stayed with him from the first watch of the hour of the rat through the third watch of the hour of the ox* but returned to her own rooms without having revealed her true feelings. The young man was greatly sad and unable to sleep the rest of the night. The next morning her silence was still on his mind, but as he could not send one of his own men to her he waited most unhappily. Well on into the morning there arrived from the Virgin Priestess's quarters nothing beyond this poem:

> Did you come to me
> or did I go out to you?
> Now I cannot tell
> was it dream or was it fact
> was I waking or sleeping. . . .

Weeping profusely the young man recited:

> Dark as night my soul
> wondering just as you do
> about yesternight—
> Whether fact or dream's fiction
> let us decide this evening!

* 2:00–2:30 A.M.

After he had it delivered he went out to hunt. He walked the moors but his heart was elsewhere—"To-night at least when all are fast asleep we shall meet at the earliest," he thought. But the Provincial Governor, also in charge of the Ise Shrine, had heard of his visit and held a wine-fest all night long, and they were unable to meet at all. Since he would have to leave for the province of Owari at the dawn, the young man too secretly shed tears of blood . . . but there could be no meeting. As the night gradually lightened to coming day there came from the Priestess's quarters a farewell cup of wine with a poem written upon the stand. The young man took it and read:

> Though one walks across
> the bay of our relations
> his cuffs remain quite dry . . .

The last two lines were missing. With some charcoal from a pine torch that was on the tray he finished the poem, writing:

> . . . Yet will I cross the Barrier
> of Meeting again, my love!

And with the day he crossed into Owari Province.

*　　*　　*

During the reign of Mizu-no-O, the Virgin Priestess was the daughter of Emperor Montoku, Prince Kore-taka's younger sister.

✦ DAN LXX

Long ago a young man returning from his mission as Imperial Falconer took lodging at the Ōyodo Ferry and sent this poem to the Virgin Priestess through her maidservant:

> Which way can I go
> to cut down the dark seaweeds
> hiding her from sight?
> Point with your oar and show me
> oh Fishing Boat of Heaven!

✦ DAN LXXI

Long ago a young man had journeyed to the Palace of the Virgin Priestess of the Ise Shrine as an Imperial Envoy. A woman serving at that palace who was a skilled conversationalist on matters of love whispered to him:

> Soul tempestuous
> even the god's sacred fence
> can be put behind—
> Just with the hope of seeing
> a noble Court personage.

And he:

> If you are inclined
> come and try me on for size!

Soul tempestuous
even the gods of heaven
would not bar the road to love.

✦ *DAN LXXII*

Long ago a young man was unable to meet for a second time a woman in Ise Province. Because he was very bitter toward her saying he was going to a neighboring province, the woman recited:

Though it is not true
that the Ōyodo pines
bear them any grudge,
laden with white hot hatred
the waves back off and recede!

✦ *DAN LXXIII*

Long ago, his thoughts directed toward a woman to whom he could not even send a letter containing his feelings though he had heard she was at a certain place, the poem:

Though I see you there
still I cannot capture you:
You are like the shadow

of the moon's great laurel tree
real yet always out of reach!

✦ *DAN LXXIV*

Long ago a young man, feeling terribly bitter toward
a woman:

> Though the barrier
> is no crag strewn mountain range
> dangerous to cross—
> Days of your rejection mount
> till my love can breathe no more!

✦ *DAN LXXV*

Long ago a young man said, "Come and live with me
in Ise Province," and the woman replied:

> Say you that there grow
> at the Ōyodo Strand
> seaweeds dark and deep?—
> My heart cannot blossom out
> in your fresh water haven.

Having thus shown even more indifference toward
him; the young man:

Sleeves drenched with the waves
goes he scything through the weeds
great god of the sea—
Having seen me but this once
you dry up like the desert?

She:

To the murky weeds
growing in among the crags
nothing seems worthwhile:
Ebbing tides nor high tides full
bring no presents from the sea!

And he:

So great are my tears
that no wringing drives them out:
Should the bitterness
that you brew within your heart
flow in drops from off my sleeve?

Indeed she was a difficult woman to get along with!

✦ *DAN LXXVI*

Long ago at a time when the Consort of the Second
Ward was still spoken of as the mother of the Heir
Apparent this lady went to perform worship before

her clan's deity. Then an old man who served in the Guard of the Inner Palace, after the others had received their rewards, was given his own reward directly from the Consort's own carriage, and in accepting this present he offered up the poem:

> Verily, today
> at this Ōhara Shrine
> and its small salt hill!
> Do they not now recollect
> the happy age of the gods . . . ?

Did he perhaps have a heart laden with sadness . . . or how must he have felt? We know not!

✦ DAN LXXVII

Long ago there lived an emperor who was known as the Tamura Emperor. Among his concubines at that time there was one called Takakiko. When she passed away sutra recitations were performed on her behalf at the Anjō Temple. The entire Court sent offerings. Altogether these came to about a thousand. These many offerings were attached to tree branches, and because it was before the main hall of the compound it appeared as though the very mountains had come nearer! Noticing this the General of the Right, a man called Fujiwara no Tsuneyuki, had all of the poets gathered after the sutras were over and made them recite poems in the mood of spring with the day's ceremonies as their topic. The Captain of the Right of the Imperial Stables who was an old man, as though his eyes were playing tricks on him, recited:

> That the mountains too
> all have drawn nigh unto us
> on this very day—
> They have come to pay respect
> at her last farewell to spring.

Such was his composition, but as we look at it now it was not worthy at all. Were there no poems better than this Captain's on that day . . . ? for they were moved by this poem of his.

✦ DAN LXXVIII

Long ago there lived a lady in the Emperor's retinue called Takakiko. She passed away and the sutra recitations of the forty-ninth day were held at the Anjō Temple. General of the Right Fujiwara no Tsuneyuki had attended, and on his way back he stopped at the Yamashina Palace of His Highness Tonsured Prince Yamashina. The palace garden had a lofty waterfall, swift watercourses quite charmingly constructed. Tsuneyuki said, "Your Grace, these long years have I served for thee at a distance and not yet waited upon you at close quarters. If it please Your

12. "*At the Yamashina Palace . . .*"   (*Dan LXXVIII*)

Grace, might I wait upon you this night. . . ." The
Prince was delighted and had a banquet ordered for
that evening. The General of the Right then withdrew
from the audience and spoke to his people in this way:
"As this is my first chance to wait upon His Highness,
how can I go without some offering? At the time of
His Majesty the Emperor's visit to the Third Ward a
rather enhancing stone from Chisato Beach in Ki
Province was to have been presented, but as it came
after His Majesty had left, we set it in a ditch before
the apartments of a certain lady. Prince Yamashina is
most fond of garden architecture so I shall present this
stone." Having spoken he sent an outrider and a
retainer to fetch it. They returned with the stone without delay. The appearance of this stone surpassed its
reputation. Thinking it would be most inelegant to
offer it just as it was, Tsuneyuki had his people compose poems. The poem of the man who was Captain
of the Right at the Imperial Stables he had written upon
the stone in the manner of lacquer inlay by cutting
away the green moss for the letters, and in this form
he presented it.

> Here upon this rock
> though it be inadequate
> do I show my hue:
> For there is no outward way
> to show you my devotion.

So ran his poem.

Long ago an Imperial Prince was born within the clan.
Clansmen recited poems in celebration of this auspi-
cious event. That composed by the old man who was
the child's great-uncle was:

> Here within our gate
> have we planted a bamboo
> with a mile long shadow—
> Who in summer or winter
> would not find rest beneath it?

     *   *   *

This was Imperial Prince Sadakazu. At that time
people said he was actually the son of the Colonel. He
was the son of the daughter of Minister of the Center
Yukihira, the Colonel's elder brother.

🔷 *DAN LXXX*

Long ago there lived a man who had planted some
wistaria at a house whose political fortunes were on the
decline. At the end of the third month on a drizzling
rainy day he broke off a spray and intending to have
them given to someone recited:

> While I got soaked through
> with good cause I plucked this spray:

I had realized
that in the course of nature
spring has but a few days left.

◆ *DAN LXXXI*

Long ago there lived a certain Minister of the Left. By
the bank of the Kamo River around the Sixth Ward
he had built his elegant mansion and there did he dwell.
Toward the end of the tenth month just after the
chrysanthemums had passed from their peak to a
gentle fading of color and the variety of the autumn
leaves seemed of a beauty unimaginable he invited the
Imperial Princes and held a wine-fest with music
throughout the night. As dawn gradually began to
break they composed poems praising the elegance of
this mansion. A beggarly old man who had attended
hobbled to below the dais, and after all the others had
made their poems he recited:

Have I somehow come
to wondrous Shiogama?
In the morning calm
could I wish that fishing boats
might even draw up to the shores . . .

* * *

As he had been to the Michi Provinces he had known

many strangely beautiful places. But none of the places within the sixty-odd provinces of the realm could match that place called Shiogama. Thus it was that the old man particularly impressed mentioned "arriving at Shiogama" in his poem.

✦ DAN LXXXII

Long ago there lived an Imperial Prince named Prince Koretaka. Just beyond Yamazaki at the place known as Minase he had a detached palace. Each year when the cherry blossoms were flowering he was to be found at that palace. On such occasions he usually took with him the man who was Captain of the Right in the Imperial Stables. (As this happened long ago I have forgotten the name of the man.) They were not too avid about falconry but rather immersed themselves in writing native-style poems while drinking great amounts of wine. The cherries at this palace, now the Nagisa Palace in the hunting region of Katano, were especially magnificent. Dismounting from their horses and sitting beneath the trees they broke off flowering sprays and wreathed themselves in blossoms. Without distinctions of rank everyone composed poems. That recited by the Captain of the Stables:

> If within this world
> there should be no cherry flowers

for all to enjoy
how would men then free of care
find their hearts in the springtime!

Such indeed was his. And someone else:

When indeed they fall
how much more these cherry flowers
are endeared to us—
What within this fleeting world
is meant to last forever . . . ?

As they got up to return the sun had already set. One of
the company who had been given to carry the wine
came up from the fields. "Let us finish off this wine,"
said he, and in looking for a suitable spot they came to
a place called River of Heaven. This Captain of the
Stables presented the chalice to the Prince. His Highness spoke, saying: "Upon the theme of having
hawked in Katano and come to the banks of the River
of Heaven you shall recite poems as you pass the cups."
Thus the Captain of the Stables recited for the Prince:

From the Weaving Maid
after a day of hunting
I would lodging seek
since we at twilight have come
to the River of Heaven.

Again and again His Highness repeated this poem but

was unable to come up with a fitting reply. Ki no Aritsune was also in attendance upon the Prince and his returning poem was:

> Only once he comes,
> she awaits the Herdsman Star
> for their yearly tryst:
> I am hard put to believe
> she'd welcome any other!

They returned then to the detached palace. Until quite late at night they were drinking and telling stories when the Prince, who was well in his cups, made to retire. Because the eleventh-night moon, too, was about to disappear, the Captain of the Stables recited:

> I would still see more
> yet the shy coquettish moon
> does absent itself?
> How I wish the mountainside
> could draw aside its curtain!

Reciting on behalf of His Highness in return, Aritsune:

> I too would desire
> all the mountain peaks alike
> leveled to the ground:
> Without such hiding places
> the moon could stand uncovered.

✦ DAN LXXXIII

Long ago the aged Captain of the Stables was serving
in the company of Prince Koretaka when he went to
Minase for his traditional hunting expedition. After a
few days the Prince returned to his Palace at the
Capital. The Captain had accompanied him thus far
and thought to return to his own home, but the Prince
was intent upon giving him his reward and some wine.
This Captain of the Stables, anxious with waiting:

> No, I shall not make
> woven grasses my pillow
> for so short a night—
> They cannot be so trusted
> as the nights when autumn reigns.

It was the last of the third month when he recited this
poem. The Prince did not retire to his bedchamber that
night but sat up until the dawn.

So it was that the old man continued to come and
serve the Prince when unexpectedly His Highness took
the tonsure of religious orders. At New Year's the
Captain decided to go and pay his respects, and coming
to Ono the snow was quite deep, as it was at the foot
of Mt. Hiei. With great difficulty he finally made his
way to the Prince's quarters. When he had paid his
respects he was aware of the oddly cold loneliness of
the place, and as the Prince was sunk in sad thoughts he
stayed for rather a long while. They talked about the
events of the past and the Captain thought to himself

how excellent it would be if he could just remain there with the Prince. But there were his many duties at the Court so he could not possibly remain. Intending to return at the dusk:

> Your robes are forgot
> and your state seems as a dream:
> Did I ever think
> there could be such snows to brave
> when I would visit my Lord?

♦ DAN LXXXIV

Long ago there lived a young man. True, he was of a low rank, but his mother was an Imperial Princess. This lady who was his mother resided in a place called Nagaoka. As this son was serving at the Court in the Capital, he was unable to pay a visit to her for long periods though he tried. As this was her only child she felt most deeply about him. So it was when just in the twelfth month there was suddenly a letter from her. He read it and was surprised to find the poem:

> As I grow in age
> that farewell which is final
> must be spoken of—
> Thus all the more I yearn now
> to see my son once again.

The son, weeping profusely, recited:

> Ah, within this world
> that farewell which is final
> I would wish away:
> For your thousandth year I pray,
> I who am your loving child.

✦ DAN LXXXV

Long ago there lived a young man. That Prince whom he had served since his childhood took the tonsure of priesthood. In the first month he of course presented himself. Because he was a public servant of the Court, this man was not usually able to get away. Nevertheless, he managed to present himself in the same way as he had always done. Those who had served the Prince in the past gathered in numbers . . . those who were still laymen, those who had become monks . . . and as it was the New Year and a special occasion the host passed round the great wine flagon. The snow fell as though it were being poured from some great vessel, and it did not stop all the day. Everyone became drunken, and there were poems on the subject of being snowed in:

> Though you be my Lord
> I cannot split into two:

Thus the driving snows
keeping me here at your side
are just what I might wish for!

When the man had recited this the Prince became most melancholy, and deeply moved he made a present of his cloak.

✦ DAN LXXXVI

Long ago a very young man made love to a very young girl. Each had parents and thus out of fear of them the romance broke off short. Several years later —was he not intending to cool her long ardor—the young man composed and had this poem delivered to the girl:

Even to today
holding such long memory
in this world there is none!
Each of us in separate ways
having passed the years between. . . .

Thus he ended the affair. Both the man and the woman entered Palace service where they were never far from each other.

◆ *DAN LXXXVII*

Long ago a young man, having some estates in Tsu Province, Mubara District, Ashiya hamlet, went there and lived. In a poem of long ago:

> At the reed dwelling
> those who make salt from the sea
> have no time to spare:
> With unloosed hair have they come,
> no time for their boxwood combs.

From such a poem comes the name of this hamlet, for it was spoken of as "the rough sea at the reed dwelling." As this young man had only superfluous duties at the Court, these could easily be put off when he went with the Palace Guards. Both this young man and his older brother had the rank of Captain of the Guard. They strolled along the sea at the front of his house and said, "Let us climb up to see the Nunobiki Falls at the top of this mountain!" And when they climbed and looked it was quite different from other waterfalls. The rock face was twenty *jō** in height and five *jō* broad, and it was indeed as thought the cliff was wrapped in white silk! At the top of these falls a rock about the size of a round straw cushion jutted out. The water which ran over this surface spilled down in pillars the size of tangerine or chestnut trees. Everyone who was there was set to making waterfall poems. That Captain of the Guard was the first to recite:

* *jō*=3.31 yd. (3.03 m.)

13. "Everyone . . . set to making waterfall poems."
    (Dan LXXXVII)

While my life may end
on the morrow or today
I cannot but wait
as I spill cascading tears . . .
which may be the greater fall?

Next to recite was the host:

There would seem to be
someone who is scattering
these watery pearls:
Do they not fall ceaselessly
on my poor and narrow sleeve?

Would not those nearby have found this amusing? . . .
with this poem they were moved and quit composing
further.

The way back was long and when they passed before
the house of the late Palace Chamberlain Mochiyoshi
the sun had set. When they looked off toward their
home they could see the many bait-lights of the fishermen, and thus the man who was their host recited:

In the clear night sky
are those fireflies by the stream
or the shining stars—
Or might they be the bait-fires
of the village fishermen?

Then they returned to the house. That night a southerly wind came up, and the waves were extremely high. The next morning the young girls of that house came out and gathered the seaweed that had floated in on the waves and carried it back to the house. The mistress of the house placed this on a table sieve, covered it with oak leaves and set this out. On a leaf the poem:

> Great god of the sea
> wreathed about his ancient head
> this treasured seaweed:
> Verily for you my Lords
> has he been so unsparing!

For the poem of a rustic does this excel or fall short?

✦ DAN LXXXVIII

Long ago when he was no longer so young certain and various friends gathered to view the moon and one among them:

> For the greater part
> let us praise the moon no more:
> Every night she sinks
> and these losses all amount
> to making each of us old!

✦ DAN LXXXIX

Long ago a man of no mean status became interested in
a woman still more noble . . . and the years passed.

> If I die of love
> love unknown to other men—
> Though there be no need
> to some god or another
> will they attribute the blame.

✦ DAN XC

Long ago to a certain indifferent person, as he continued to occupy his mind with thoughts of meeting
her—will she not have felt sorry for him—: "Ah well,
tomorrow I might give you audience . . ." said she, and
with unbridled joy tinged with fears that she might go
back on her word, to a charming spray of cherry
flowers he attached:

> These cherry flowers
> bloom today so charmingly
> giving such perfume
> but, alas, for morrow's eve
> no promise of their staying!

Will she not have been of the same mind . . . ?

✦ DAN XCI

Long ago a man who lamented the conscious passing
of time, toward the end of the third month:

> Even though I mourn
> that the spring should have its end
> more so then today
> when the setting of the sun
> becomes the final curtain!

✦ DAN XCII

Long ago though he returned having come with his
love for her all he could do was to write to the woman
in a love note:

> Rowing near the reeds
> a small boat with no gunnels
> time and time again
> crosses only to return
> while no one notes the voyage. . . .

✦ DAN XCIII

Long ago a man though of low station fell in love

with an incomparable woman. Could he not expect some small reward for his love . . . ? for he thought of her lying down and as he got up and dying with love recited:

> Rank equaling rank
> ought I bear another love:
> How ridiculous
> that the love of high and low
> should bring with it so much pain!

Long ago were such things to be seen in the nature of man?

✦ *DAN XCIV*

Long ago there lived a man. How might it have come about . . . ? he no longer lived with her. Though she later got another husband there had been a child from the previous man, and therefore—though with little cordiality—he occasionally sent her letters. Since the woman was a person fond of pictures and painting, he asked that she send him one of her drawings, but as her present man was with her she did not comply for one or two days. The man, thinking this most unkind, tauntingly wrote: "That which I have asked for has not yet been given me—this of course is to be expected . . . and so is my bitterness . . ." and had this delivered with a poem. It was the autumn.

On an autumn night
the spring day is forgotten
is this not the case?
Does not the haze of autumn
far surpass the springtime mists?

Such was his poem; and the woman's reply:

A thousand autumns
would they so nearly equal
just a single spring?
Yet fall leaves and spring flowers
both in the end are scattered . . .

✦ DAN XCV

Long ago there lived a man who served the Consort of
the Second Ward. He regularly had contact with one
of her ladies, and he tried to win her favors. "Somehow
you should give me audience even from without your
curtains that I might speak to you what I feel and ease
my heart . . ." said he, and reluctantly she consented
and they met. After much talk, the man:

More than Herdsman Star's
is the love I bear for you:
River of Heaven
quick remove the barrier
keeping us so far apart!

14. " 'Somehow you should give me audience . . .' "
    (Dan XCV)

She was pleased by this poem and gave him his way.

❧ DAN XCVI

Long ago there lived a man. He passed many months trying in various ways to win a woman. As she was not made of wood or stone might she not have felt sorry for him? and little by little she thought compassionately of him. At that time, as it was just the middle of the sixth month, one or two boils broke out on the woman's body. She sent around this note:

> "Now I have no feelings at all for this meeting. An ulceration or two have appeared on my body, and what is more the weather is too terribly hot. Anon when the fall breezes begin to blow we shall meet by all means . . ."

Such was her message. As she awaited the coming of autumn there was gossip from here and there that she was to be spirited away to that person's place. Consequently, her older brother quite suddenly came to fetch her. Thus, this woman had a bough of the first autumn maples gathered, recited this poem and wrote it on the leaves to be sent:

> Wait until the fall
> was the promise that I made

> which cannot come true—
> How like a shallow inlet
> blanketed in fallen leaves!

This she left behind, saying, "If someone is sent from there, deliver this," and off she went. Well, from that moment up to today we know no more. Was she all right? in bad straits? Not even where she went do we know. The man clapped the backs of his hands together in bringing down a curse. How horrid a thing! The curses wrought by others—are they carried out or sloughed off? It was said: "Now we shall see!"

♦ DAN XCVII

Long ago there lived a certain Horikawa Minister. The celebration of his fortieth year was held at a house in the Ninth Ward, and on that day the old man who was Colonel:

> Oh, cherry blossoms,
> scatter randomly about
> in clouds of petals
> that the paths of greater age
> may be lost unto our eyes!

✤ DAN XCVIII

Long ago there lived a certain Grand Prime Minister.
A man who was in his service, just in the ninth month,
attached a pheasant to an artificial branch of plum and
had it delivered with the poem:

> On whom I depend
> you my Lord—yes, for your sake
> did I break this bough:
> To know no season's difference
> is indeed a thing quite rare!

Because such was the poem, the Minister was immensely delighted and gave the messenger a reward.

✤ DAN XCIX

Long ago, on the day of the archery contest on the
paddock of the Right Division of the Inner Guards, in
a carriage placed on the opposite side he could faintly
see a woman's face behind the bamboo shades, and thus
the man who was the Colonel recited and sent over:

> Not that I can't see you
> but that I can't see you well:
> With a yearning heart

should I daydream all this day
without any good reason?

The reply:

Whether known or not?
How then without good reason
could you draw the line
when it is but love alone
that walks the straight and narrow?

Later he came to know who she was.

✦ DAN C

Long ago a man, when he crossed over between the
Great Hall and the Kōrō Hall . . . someone from the
apartments of a very noble lady said, "Haven't you
confused forgetting grass with the passion weed?" and
when she had some handed out he received it and
recited:

Like a field in which
grow clumps of forgetting grass
I appear, and yet
this in truth is passion weed
as I will show you later!

伊勢物語

Long ago there lived a certain Arihara no Yukihira who was Captain of the Right Division of the Military Guard. Hearing there was good wine at his house, the Auditor of the Left, his superior, Fujiwara no Masachika, was being feasted by this Captain on a certain day as the guest of honor. As the host was a man of refinement, he had had an arrangement of flowers set out. Among these flowers was an unusual wistaria. Its clusters were three and one-half feet long. Making this flower the theme they recited poems. Toward the end of the recitations a brother of the host—who had come since he had heard of the captain's party—was taken by the sleeve and urged to compose. Since he claimed to know nothing of poetry he tried to decline but was pressed at last into reciting:

> At this flower's base
> hidden in obscurity
> are many great men—
> Greater than were seen hereto
> shadows the wistaria casts!

"Why have you said this?" they demanded, to which he answered: "The Grand Prime Minister is at the flowering of his career, and thus the Fujiwara Clan is enjoying great success." Everyone ceased his criticism.

✦ DAN CII

Long ago there lived a man. Though he did not compose poems he was quite familiar with the ways of love. A noble lady became a nun and seeking to forsake the bitter world did not even stay in the Capital but lived rather in a distant mountain hamlet. Since she was originally from his clan this man recited and sent:

> Though you spurn the world
> yours is not a saintliness
> which might mount the clouds—
> Yet the sorrows of this life
> are leaving you to solace.

*   *   *

This was the Virgin Priestess.

✦ DAN CIII

Long ago there lived a man. He was very honest and sincere and not of a fickle nature. He served Emperor Fukakusa. Had he not committed an indiscretion in making love to a woman who was in service to the Imperial Princes? Well, he recited and sent:

> As our night of love
> seemed as fleeting as a dream—
> How much more, my love,

does it appear a phantom
as I doze off once again . . . !

What a sordid poem!

✦ *DAN CIV*

Long ago without there being any special circumstances there was a woman who became a nun. Though
she dressed herself in the suitable way would she not
have longed to appear better? for in going to the Kamo
Festival a man recited this poem and sent it to her:

> With her world the sea
> the fishing girl can but gather
> her dreary seaweeds—
> But when she comes to market
> still would I purchase her goods.

*   *   *

It is said this was recited near the carriage where the
Virgin Priestess was sightseeing and that upon hearing
this she cut short her stay.

✦ *DAN CV*

Long ago a young man said, "Just as I am I might die

of love . . ." and sent this off, to which a woman answered:

> If the lustrous dew
> must vanish then so be it—
> But should it remain
> there need not be anyone
> who strings the white beads as pearls.

Because such was her poem he thought her terribly rude, but his love for her still continued to grow.

✦ DAN CVI

Long ago a man, coming to where the Imperial Princes were amusing themselves, at the bank of Dragon Field River:

> Wondrous to behold
> the Age of Gods never saw this:
> Dragon Field River
> all its waters dyed somehow
> to a deep Chinese crimson!

✦ DAN CVII

Long ago there lived a noble man. A girl who was in

this man's service was courted by a man named Fujiwara no Toshiyuki who was one of the Court Scrive-
ners. Nevertheless, because she was still young, she
could not write exact letters and did not know how to
speak properly—needless to say poem making was out
of the question. So the man who was head of the house
wrote a draft, made her copy it out and sent this off.
Toshiyuki was visibly impressed. Well, he recited:

> All alone in thought
> staring thickly as the rains:
> Swollen Stream of Tears
> drenches me up to my sleeves
> for I cannot meet my love. . . .

As usual in such matters the man replied in place of
the girl:

> Shallow it is sure
> if none but your sleeves was soaked:
> Swollen Stream of Tears
> I would find reliable
> if I heard you'd floated off.

Such was the poem that the suitor was so greatly
moved that it is said indeed that even today it is still
rolled up and kept in a letter box. He sent a letter back.
After she had received this the following happened.
". . . as it seems likely to rain, I am in a quandary as to
what to do. If luck is with me, this storm may not come

after all . . ." wrote he, and again the man in place of the girl recited this poem to be delivered:

> It is hard to ask
> if you love me or do not
> time and time again—
> The rains which know my fortune
> fall with ever growing strength.

So without either raincoat or umbrella her lover came over in great perplexity, soaked through to the skin!

✦ DAN CVIII

Long ago a woman, hating a certain man's fickle nature:

> Is it that the wind
> blows the whitecaps still higher
> over these rough crags
> that the sleeves of my garment
> are always drenched with their foam?

But, hearing himself that she customarily recited such things the man:

> Every single night
> in the rice fields the bullfrogs

cry themselves quite dry—
Thus the waters are increased
even without the rainfall!

✤ *DAN CIX*

Long ago a man sent to the residence of a friend who
had lost his wife:

More than any flower
the life of your beloved
has been so fleeting:
Which, my friend, would you have thought
the harbinger of your grief?

✤ *DAN CX*

Long ago a man had a woman he visited secretly. From
her came the note: "You have appeared in my dreams
this night . . ." so the man recited:

With so fierce a love
that my spirit on its own
wandered to your side—
Should it come in deeper night
overcome it with magic!

✦ *DAN CXI*

Long ago a man, as though he were consoling her over the death of a maidservant, wrote to a lady of high birth:

> In the ages past
> could such things have existed?
> Now indeed I know
> that a person never seen
> may be the object of love!

She replied:

> My silk trouser cord
> though it be a love symbol
> has not come untied—
> The speech you have made is false
> as it is void of love's deeds.

And he again:

> That I am in love
> is more than I meant to say:
> If your trouser cord
> ever should become untied
> be kind enough to call me . . .

✤ *DAN CXII*

Long ago a man because a woman who had devoutly
promised herself to him was now of a different mind:

> Suma fishermen
> burning salt—the smoke billows:
> As the winds blow full
> it goes gently trailing off
> to an unthought of quarter.

✤ *DAN CXIII*

Long ago a man was for the time living alone:

> Ah, how brief it is . . .
> yet this life can encompass
> my being forgot:
> Then how sadly circumscribed
> that heart without a memory . . .

✤ *DAN CXIV*

Long ago on the occasion when Emperor Ninna made
his outing to Serikawa, though he thought such things

were no longer suited to him an old man served as Imperial Falconer for the great falcons as he had once been connected with this post. On the sleeve of his mottled hawking gown he wrote:

> Though so old a man
> do not think the less of me
> for my gay attire:
> It is only for the day
> that the crane cries so loudly.

The Emperor appeared displeased. Though the old man had been thinking of his own advanced age, it seems His Majesty—no longer so young—took it to mean himself, does it not?

✦ *DAN CXV*

Long ago in the Province of Michi a man and woman lived together. "I shall be going to the Capital," said the man. The woman was very saddened and offered at the least to make a farewell party; at the place called Capital Island of Okinoite she gave him the wine to drink and recited:

> Charcoal embers red
> burn my body—nonetheless
> what is more unkind

is this parting at the shore
of this Capital Island.

✦ DAN CXVI

Long ago a man with no special purpose wandered all
the way to Michi Province. To a person in the Capital
he was thinking of he sent:

> From among the waves
> I can see a small island
> with the huts' thatch eaves:
> It has been so awfully long
> that I have been without you . . .

". . . Everything has changed for the better," he wrote!

✦ DAN CXVII

Long ago His Majesty made an outing to Sumiyoshi:

> Since I saw them first
> much time has fled the present—
> At Sumiyoshi
> maiden pines upon the beach
> what ages have they lived through?

A great and august god made himself manifest:

> You are close to me
> as the white waves—you should know
> that my sacred fence
> in most high antiquity
> began to guard your household.

✦ *DAN CXVIII*

Long ago a man after a long period of silence said, "My heart has not forgotten you. May I call upon you . . . ?" So she sent back:

> Lovely languorous vine
> you have got so many trees
> round which you entwine—
> Thus that you should be constant
> plants no joy within my heart.

✦ *DAN CXIX*

Long ago a woman looking at some things left behind as souvenirs by a rather unreliable man:

> Souvenirs indeed . . .
> now become my enemies!

15. *"Looking at some things left behind as souvenirs . . ."*
    (Dan CXIX)

Were it not for these
there could be a few moments
when at last I could forget. . . .

✤ DAN CXX

Long ago a man thought a woman had no experience of men, but heard she had secretly pledged herself
to another and later recited:

Let the time be soon
when the Tsukuma Feast-Day
comes to Ōmi:
I'd see how many stewpots
a heartless wench can gather!

✤ DAN CXXI

Long ago a man, on seeing someone withdrawing from
the Plum Blossom Apartments soaked with the rain:

They say the brown thrush
sews a hat of plum blossoms—
This I wish for you
seemingly so drenched with rain
to wear as you go homeward.

[154]

The reply:

> True the nightingale
> sews a rainhat of blossoms—
> But instead of this
> give me the fire of passion
> to dry me as I go home.

✦ DAN CXXII

Long ago a man to a person who had been contrary to her promised word:

> In Yamashiro
> the clear waters of Ide
> slip right through my hands:
> No good are your promises
> poured in a bottomless cup!

Thus he recited, but there was no reply.

✦ DAN CXXIII

Long ago there lived a man. Did he not gradually become tired of a woman living in Tall Grasses Village? for he recited this poem:

For these many years
my home has been this village—
If I go away
more and more the tall grasses
will become a wilderness . . .

The woman answered:

If this place grows wild
I would then become a quail
crying on that moor—
Even if only sometimes
would you not come here hunting?

He was moved by such composition and lost the desire
to leave her.

✦ DAN CXXIV

Long ago a man—of what things might he have been
thinking on a certain occasion?—recited:

My own secret thoughts
I shall tell to no one else—
That will be the best
as there is no other soul
wholly equal to my own.

16. *"As he knew in his heart that he was to die . . ."*
    (Dan CXXV)

✦ *DAN CXXV*

Long ago a man fell gravely ill, and as he knew in his heart that he was to die . . . :

> In the end—this road
> deathward all men must travel:
> This I always knew
> but yesterday or today . . .
> no! never had I thought it.

NOTES TO THE TRANSLATION

Since the main purpose of this volume is the presentation of *Ise-monogatari* as a work of literature, notes within the body of the text have been kept to an absolute minimum. These notes are appended to guide the reader informally into a deeper understanding of not only the novel itself but the whole of what it is that makes this literature intrinsically Japanese. I have consciously avoided dwelling on points of grammar, etymology, *variae lexiones,* etc., as this work is well handled in English in the Vos translation. Rather, these notes deal with matters of cultural interest and problems of translation.

For those readers without a knowledge of Japanese I can highly recommend the two volumes of the Vos translation; those readers with a Japanese background who wish to go further will find most useful the works by Ōtsu and the late Dr. Ikeda.

DAN I: In this first episode, the hero attains manhood, which we may specify as having occurred between twelve and fifteen years of age, and he goes hunting at one of the family estates. The ladies he observes from a distance and secretly, as Heian society tabooed all direct informal contact between the sexes. The reference to the "old city" is easily explained; this is Nara, the capital until 784. Nara was never fully developed and so was easily regarded as in its decline. We should note, however, that the new capital of Heian—now Kyoto—was itself hardly begun.

The cutting of the cuff and sending it with the poem is a specific instance of the manner in which casual love letters were exchanged. Here, the dyed pattern of the cloth is the clue to the meaning of the pun in the original Japanese. Further, the citation of an earlier poem—here interpolated by a later editor—is a second device to reinforce the image of the whole episode.

"Elegance" is the literal meaning of *miyabi,* the first of several aesthetic concepts intrinsic to any understanding of Japanese literature. It is variously translated as "courtliness," "grandeur," etc., but the central concept to be grasped lies in the social structure of this period. Society equaled the aristocracy, an aristocracy which had grown out of extended alliances with the Imperial household. The elegance of *miyabi* lies in the languorous beauty, pomp and ceremony of the Court, and the lives of those who serve it within the capital itself; beyond the physical limits of Heian *miyabi* could be no more than a reflection of the true aesthetic sense.

DAN II: Here in the second episode we have *miyabi* in its proper setting; the western half of Heian was unfinished, thus lending an air of loneliness to the general context. The season is identified as spring—with the reference being to the old lunar calendar—in the poem by the pun on *naga-*

meru, to sit staring off into the distance, and *naga-ame,* the characteristic spring rains. The composition of a love poem on the morning after a tryst—usually shortly after arriving back home—was not a pleasantry but an unbreakable norm of social conduct.

DAN III: The reader may already note the standardization—almost complete throughout the tale—of the first sentence; this not only typifies *Ise* as an episodic work but, further, goes far to aid the stereotyping and symbolization of the main character.

The introductory prose is no more than an explanation of the poem, there being a pun between *hijikimo,* "duckweed," and *hijiki-mono,* "bedding." As mentioned above, the sending of such things as cloth, flowers, etc., was as a clue to the involved meanings of the poem. While "duckweed" is not an exact correspondence in English, the pun is accomplished and one can visualize the thick but soft and delicate plant growing at the edge of the water near the poet's simple cottage.

A later historical interpolation links Narihira, the original poet, with Fujiwara no Takako. This woman became first Consort and then Empress to Emperor Seiwa; her affair with Narihira caused them both much trouble and great pain, as may be deduced from later episodes.

DAN IV: Historical fact comes more to the fore in this episode though great care has been taken to generalize the hero and his amours; in the name of fairness to *Ise* as a novel, then, we need not worry about the specifics of Narihira and Takako, which interpretations after all are of a later date than the novel *per se*. More important is that we notice the delicacy with which the characters handle themselves. The hero, knowing his goal cannot be realized, is nevertheless unable to contain his emotions, while the girl, anticipating his rashness, avoids the meeting by going away. Moreover, we have the subtle beginnings of this love affair expressed, without a statement, by the season, the beginning of spring and new life characteristically symbolized in the blossoming of the plum. The faintness of this aesthetic beauty so deeply felt is obvious in the dramatic interval of a year between the original visit and the composition of the poem.

This poem is one of the more famous in *Ise* and most frequently interpreted. The grammar lends itself to opposing views of the relationship between man and nature. The translation is designed to yield either of these interpretations.

DAN V: The reference to the Fifth Ward (*gojō*) easily lends to the later interpolation of the Narihira-Takako relationship because of the use of geographical locations of palaces, mansions, etc. as oblique metaphors replacing personal names. The Dowager Empress, Fujiwara no Junshi, lived in a palace in the *gojō* district. (This practice also utilized court positions: the name of the author of the *Tale of Genji* is used by Waley as the prime example of such usage.)

In the social atmosphere of Heian the visits of a man to a lady's chambers were supposed to be secretly executed; but what with all of his outriders, retainers, and bodyguards and all her maids and ladies-in-waiting, "secret" could only indicate the lack of clear light and the absence of the commotion of being formally announced.

DAN VI: The historical interpolations, as suggested above, should not be used as guides for interpreting the main segments of the text. It is most valuable, however, to use these passages comparatively for an understanding of the meaning of *Ise* in context of the period of composition. Here we see a definite contradiction between the text and the interpolation. The latter would have us understand the girl to be Takako. But: could an intended empress possibly be abducted? could she be so naïve as not to know dew when she saw it? Further, belief in demons who devour people is clearly of folk origin; and so courtly a man as Narihira would hardly "stamp his feet in grief!" Surely, the main text of this episode takes a poem by Narihira as its base and cleverly weaves a story from earlier folk materials. The textual key which opens the way for the forced historical interpolation is the river called Akutagawa. The referent of the folk sources is to a river in the Mishima area of Osaka, but there was also a small man-made stream of the same name within the grounds of the Heian Imperial Palace.

DAN VII: The only note here is the pun of "mounting" and mountain—unstated—the latter, *yama,* included in the former *urayamashi*. The physical scene was a favorite of woodblock artists and most particularly Hokusai.

DAN VIII: This episode continues the hero's travels in the Eastern Provinces (from Kyoto to Tokyo) which may historically have been Narihara's voluntary exile because of the affair with Takako, though there is no clear historical record of such an exile.

DAN IX: The central point of interest in the first section of this episode is, of course, the acrostic poem which—due to the language structure of the original—was syllabic in Japanese. "Flags" corresponds to the Japanese *kakitsubata* used as the acrostic; but the many devices of Japanese prosody are also used, thus making a most complex poem. Consequently, this poem is a good subject for detailed analysis of the subtleties of Japanese poetry.

In transliteration the original runs as follows:

> KAragoromo
> KItsutsu narenishi
> TSUma shi areba
> HA*rubaru kinuru
> TAbi o shi zo omou

The first line indicates the court dress modeled on that of the T'ang Dynasty in China; it also may refer, therefore, to the person wearing it. *Kitsutsu* means "while wearing" and "while traveling"; *narenishi* is both "having become accustomed to" and "having become soiled." *Tsuma* means "the skirt of a garment" and "wife"; *haru,* "to stretch and block out a garment" and "as far as this"; *kinuru,* "had worn" and "had traveled." Each of these words "pivots" to yield more than one meaning and is thus a pivot-word

---

* In the classical writing system the syllables HA, BA, and PA were represented by one grapheme distinguished by context only.

(*kakekotoba*); moreover, all of them after the first line make a string of "related words" (*engo*) with double meanings. To all of this is added the device of the acrostic.

We might also note in passing the comic (folk) nature of the sentence after the poem ending the first segment of this episode. The same type of statement occurs again in the last sentence of the episode as a whole.

The second of the four parts of this episode continues the eastward journey. The pun on Mt. Utsu and the literal meaning of *utsu*, "reality," operates in both the prose and the poetry. The image of melting patches of snow, the central picture of the third section, is rich in its beauty, but, as this locale was mostly unfamiliar to the residents of Heian, a concrete reference of explanatory nature is added. This should be a clue to the broad sphere of interest of the readers as it contrasts with the limited scope of their experiential knowledge.

The last segment of this episode may perhaps have roots in folk sources, considering the comic nature of the ferryman;* the fact that the aristocrats had never seen a seagull, however, is wholly reasonable what with their limited experiences outside of the capital city itself. The pun is on *miyakodori*, "gull," which is composed of *miyako*, "capital," and *tori*, "bird."

---

* It is also possible that the comical description is generated more simply by a lack of understanding of or experience with anyone not of the aristocracy. A good example of this type of description is found in the *Pillow Book* (Sei Shōnagon, *The Pillow Book of Sei Shōnagon*, trans. Arthur Waley [New York: Grove Press, 1960], pp. 83–84).

DAN X: There are two things of note in this episode: namely, the social meaning of being an aristocrat and the translation of this into poetry. The mother of the girl involved had been unalterably disgraced by having become the wife of a commoner, most especially since she was of the rising Fujiwara clan. Her relationship to that clan, therefore, obligated her to seek for her daughter a better marriage than she herself had made. The marriage customs of Heian Japan were rooted in the remains of a matriarchal system operant in a patriarchal society (though this patriarchy was often only *de jure*). For a detailed discussion of these customs see chapter 8 (pp. 199–250) of Ivan Morris's *The World of the Shining Prince* (New York: Knopf, 1964).

The goal of an aristocratic marriage is translated into the meaning of the poem, but, more than that, the mother's need to vindicate herself is seen in her posturing as her daughter, who would have been the proper author of such a poem. In the returning poem, the hero demonstrates another of the meanings of aristocracy. We assume that he is of course aware of the mother's disgrace. Thus his mere rearrangement of her words into an ambiguous answer shows on the one hand his contempt for the mother and on the other the complete casualness with which he conducts affairs that can have no measurable value to his political and social life within the capital. There is no callousness involved in these attitudes, as their converses could not be conceptualized.

DAN XI: The only interesting point in this episode deals with the establishment of a possible date of composition for the novel. The *Shūishū,* an anthology compiled by Imperial order in 1001, has this poem attributed to Tachibana no Tadamoto, who died while he was Governor of Suruga Province in 957.

DAN XII: The poem in this episode is a reworking of one found in the *Manyōshū* (*ca.* 750), the earliest anthology of Japanese poetry. As a whole, then, this is another type of insertion of folk materials. In writing the preparatory prose, however, the author leaves what may be a trace of the original format of Narihara's poetic diary; the facts are stated—by Narihira, I suggest—in the first sentence. What prose follows this is an elaboration through flashback done by the author.

In the poem, "young grasses" (*wakakusa*) is what is known —together with the particle *no*—as a pillow-word (*makurakotoba*). The *makurakotoba* is a prosodic device standardized by the *Manyōshū* poets whereby a phrase is solidified into a standard metaphor which is suppletive in nature. That is, it does not replace its referent but is antecedent to its occurrence; without the referent it has no prosodic existence.

DAN XIII: Beauty as a cult and its relation to belles-lettres is described at length by Morris (chapters 7 and 8). We are concerned in this episode with *miyabi* through the device of using "Musashi Stirrups" metaphorically and as a key to the poems. If the hero merely intended to indicate his location, Musashi would have sufficed; the "stirrups" is the key to the involved *engo* of the poem he "could have" sent but did not, as well as indicating a district in Musashi noted for its manufacture of lacquer stirrups. In the woman's poem the phrase as a whole (*musashi abumi*) is a *makurakotoba* for

[167]

kakeru, "to hang, attach, put on." In the original this is complicated by the insertion of *sasugani,* "indeed, however," which also means the pin by which the stirrup is attached to the saddle. Thus the use of "toss" for *kakeru* in the translation might let the reader envision the reslinging of the stirrups after tightening the cinch in preparation for riding off (deserting the woman). The metaphor is then carried through in the man's poem in the double use of "horn" for both dilemma and the pommel of a saddle. The *miyabi* lies not so much in knowing all this but in apprehending it and thus granting to the individual author of the emotion his great skill in subtle expression.

DAN XIV: With this episode in Michi we have the shift to the "northern leg" of the hero's travels. As explained earlier and exemplified here, the farther one went from the capital the less *miyabi* was to be found. If the woman was stunned by the magnificence of a Court noble, he must have been equally shaken by the rustic crudeness evident in her two poems. This brings us to the concept of *hinabi* or *inakabi,* both of which may be translated as "rustic, countrified air." As one aesthetic concept, these words signify not so much the polar opposites of *miyabi* as a provincial misinterpretation and vain striving for all that *miyabi* signifies.

The woman's first poem is, simply, bad poetry—and is translated as such; her use of *tama no o* (literally, "the space between strung pearls") as a poeticism for "short" is, while correct, ineffective because her metaphor is unstructured. Her second poem is so *hinabi* that the nicest thing we can call it is crude! The segment "drown him in the washtub" could also mean "feed him to the foxes" (admitting dialectical etymologies), but this is hardly an elegant usage of the pun. "Dirty old rooster" could have been translated as "goddamn rooster" had the poet been a man.

Greatest of this woman's many faults, however, is that she misunderstood the hero's poem; she missed the nuance which—in the translation—lies in "knick-knack." In addition to the image of a gawky pine tree, the man's poem— in certain manuscripts—has a pun on the place name: as Kuwahara it could be both "mulberry plain," referring back to her "silkworm" poem, and the passive/causative stem of "to eat," noting her pun mentioned above. This is, however, tenuous, as it assumes the hero's knowledge of dialect.

DAN XV: There is a standard pun in the poem between *shinobu*, "desire," and *shinobu*, "to do secretly"; in addition, however, the use of the word *oku*, "deep recesses," may be an elegant reference to the general geographical area.

What is most significant about this episode is the way in which the woman contrasts with the lady who preceded her. This woman was of noble birth but married to a commoner; her redemption is that she recognizes the loss of *miyabi* and its replacement by *hinabi*.

DAN XVI: In this episode we have the first reference to an historical figure: Ki no Aritsune. Aritsune was in fact minister to three emperors before he was swept under by the rising tide of Fujiwara dominance at the Court; in his case, his nephew (see below, LXXIX) was replaced as Heir Apparent by the grandson of Fujiwara no Yoshifusa, the first of that clan to consolidate *de facto* ruling powers. More importantly, Aritsune was Narihira's father-in-law. Thus, in telling us that the letter was to "a friend" the author has consciously set up a fiction in which his symbolized hero must operate.

The puns on "counting" are easily achieved, but in the third poem there is a pun which I was unable to translate: *ama*, "heaven," also means "nun." The link between "dew" and "tears" in the last poem is a stock simile.

DAN XVII: In later eras "flower" will have become synonymous with "cherry" unless specified otherwise. The fact that both are used here does not show redundancy but rather indicates an age when the elaborate structures (synonymous in classical Japan with strictures) of society had not solidified—an age, I suggest, more properly attributed to Narihira than to the author of *Ise*.

The evanescence of the cherry blossom is a well-known Japanese theme; the twist in the woman's poem is her adoption of a telescoped metaphor. The man's response implies that had he not come when he did she would have either scorned him altogether or received him with much less affection. The poetic exchange of this episode characterizes well the intricacies of Heian courtship.

DAN XVIII: The underlying meaning of the first poem is that the man is rumored to be quite a lover, but that this "color" of his personality seems hidden as though he were a snow-covered branch. His reply is in answer to her riddle about the color of the chrysanthemum, a metaphor on the crimson-lined sleeve of her gown. The chrysanthemum's petals begin to turn a deep crimson at the edges as it fades;

also, on some varieties, this coloring is matched by a faint darkening of the center of the flower.

DAN XIX: The metaphor of the clouds and mountains, explicit in the second poem and implicit in the first, is comparable to the song of the king in *The King and I*, where the woman is stationary like the mountain, but the man drifts like the clouds from one peak to the next. Because the gales are so strong "on that peak which once was mine," not only is the hero driven away but also other clouds certainly will have been drawn toward it. The classical Japanese concept of clouds has them gathered around a mountain peak. In cosmological terms as well the idea of "changing partners" is evident, for the sun was to favor first the east and then the west as the day progressed; as it did so the winds came up and the clouds moved from the mountains in the east to others in the west.

DAN XX: The man's poem was meant to convey the idea that although their love affair was outwardly in its spring his feelings were like a maple aflame in autumn. The woman's poem shows she has misread his meaning; she thinks his gift of leaves whose color has changed too early means his affections too have shifted.

The use of the word *iro,* "color," in Japanese is rather complex. Besides referring to the spectrum it means rank, mood, facial expression, tone, emotion, love, lust, passion (and the full range of psycho-sexual feelings), comportment, and beauty—to list a few. Of course, the English language, too, has words with extremely broad semantic fields. The difference lies in the fact that the connotative function in

Japanese is almost entirely subjugated to the denotative; that is, *iro* is always used within the context of its full semantic range of meaning, unrestricted by context or idiom as "color" would be in English.

DAN XXI: The exchange of poems in this episode shows another aspect of Heian social relations. First we have a cryptic poem from the woman which fits well the mystery that prompted her departure. The next two poems by the hero demonstrate, in their overstatement, the emotionalism so typical of the self-centered men who filled the Court. In the second of these I have translated the *makurakotoba* literally as "jeweled hairpin" (*tamakazura*) including the word which receives it, "pierce," in order to effect the melodramatic tone reminiscent of Oedipus for just this reason. In the four poems which attempt a reconciliation we need only note "forgetting grass," *wasuregusa,* contact with which was believed to be an herbal cause of forgetting, and the use of the mountain/cloud images (see above, XIX).

Another interesting point is that it is the woman who leaves. Ownership in this period was still of a matriarchal nature, with the men going to the homes owned by their wives. The only possible explanations of this woman's actions are that she returned to her mother's home or went off to lead a homeless life.

DAN XXII: Just as the last episode depicted estrangement, so this episode shows us a reconciliation; the juxtaposition of the two is interesting. It is nearly impossible to say why the author has made the connection, but the poems are technical instruments of both developments. As the estrangement of the previous episode grows more permanent so the poems seem disconnected—especially the last two the first two poems of this reconciliation, however, play on the idea of emotional love while the second two are clearly related in content as a call-response (my own term for structurally similar *uta* and *kaeshi-uta* together).

In the second poem of the episode there is a pun on *kawashima,* "a river island," and *kawashi,* a word meaning "exchange" but here probably referring to a sexual relationship. The directness of the second line is an attempt to suggest this as politely as the original has it.

In the call-response we see an example of the Japanese interpretation of the concept of number. Chinese specifies numbers almost incalculable to the Western mind for use in descriptions of the Buddhist heavens and the various realms of the universe; to the Chinese mind these are exact numbers—for example, the *man* of *manyōshū* would literally specify a quantity of 10,000. The translation of this anthology as one of "myriad leaves" correctly catches the Japanese concept of generalized quantification. The difference seems slight, but the off-handedness of the Japanese thought-pattern helps to explain the way in which all the Chinese culture imported was contemporarily understood.

DAN XXIII: General scholarly acceptance of 950 as a tentative date for the composition of *Ise* makes it difficult to understand how so highly developed and sustained a work as *Genji* could have been written only half a century later. From varied sources we know of many other works no longer extant which are assumed to have been examples of the intervening stages of prose development. The prose of *Ise* is widely regarded as severely limited, but I suggest that the fictional scope of this episode—and others which I will point out later on—shows sufficient development to warrant considering this work as valid fiction rather than as a group of poems pasted together with infantile prose. This is not to say that *Ise* in any way equals the art of *Genji*, for their basic natures are different, though these differences cannot properly be explained within the context of these notes.

The first poem in this episode employs alliteration in the original which we should note for some basic understanding of the phonological potential of a language whose poetry does not employ rhyme. In transliteration the original is as follows:

> *TSUTSUITSU no*
> *IZUTSU ni kakeshi*
> *maro ga take*
> *suginikerashi na*
> *imo mizaru ma ni*

The use of /b,r,l/ in the translation is an attempt to give some sense of the consonance in the first two lines. The underlining above shows further consonance and assonance which I have not attempted to specifically reproduce in the English.

The "childish hair" mentioned in the second poem was the hairstyle for children of both sexes. The hair was parted in the middle and swept back to either side where it was cut at shoulder length. Boys had this cut as part of the ceremony of attaining manhood while girls had it tied up when they were married.

The third poem is a good example of the *jō* (preface) device of poetry. In this case the preface extends through the first two lines; "mounting" (*tatsu*) is part of line three (*tatsutayama*). The play between "mounting" and "mountain" besides being the pivot of the *jō* also gives the effect of a brewing storm, an atmosphere tense with danger, literal and figurative.

Characterization in this episode is particularly well handled. In the poem just discussed the mountain barrier is viewed by the faithful wife from one side as she even prays for her husband's safety as he goes to his mistress. In the next poem—the fourth—the mistress views the same mountain from the other side. She is evidently wealthy and this is her only virtue; when the hero has spent most of her money the enchantment disappears. The image of her serving herself shows her basic unattractiveness and her inability to afford a maid any longer. If the hero truly has merely used her, we can understand the grasping quality evident in the last poem.

DAN XXIV: The prolonged fiction of this episode, too, puts it on the level of prose development just discussed. The setting is not quite as provincial, *katainaka* meaning an area not immediately accessible to the capital city.

In the first poem the first line is a *makurakotoba* for "years." In order to achieve the tone of the original I have joined the adverb "darkly" with "lump" and "unpolished." The use of "pillowed" refers both to the jade as a gem and the woman in the consummation of her new marriage.

Both Ikeda and Ōtsu cite a *kagura* or Shinto ceremonial song as the source for the second poem. For the purpose of

伊勢物語

interpreting the aesthetic purport of this episode, however, I see the images as follows: The warrior's bow—made of the catalpa, spindletree, and zelkova woods (*azusa, ma, tsuki*)—is always kept at his side, which is also the place of a faithful wife. Such had been their relationship before he had been called to a higher military duty. *Ma* and *tsuki* also mean "true" and "hit a target" respectively, showing a bow which shoots straight and true. The use of "trials" also carries through the idea of a military code of personal relationships. All this imagery is maintained in the third poem even though the "longbow" (*azusayumi*) here is a *makurakotoba* for "draw"; this last word is retained in the next poem to sustain the imagery even further, though most of the atmosphere intended has already begun to ebb by this point in the original.

Though there is no clear statement of suicide in the close of the episode, suicide notes written in blood are common in later literature. In fact, this passage might lend sociological evidence for the antiquity of such a custom. The last sentence, too, is highly interesting; *itazura* as an adverbial state means "to die," but as a noun it means "illicit love." This possibly could indicate that her suicide note was merely a pose and that she returned to the second husband. On the other hand, this could be stretching the text too far under the influence of nonsynchronic semantics.

DAN XXV: The man's poem employs another stock metaphor, that of the long sleeve drenched in dew; dew is of course a substitute for tears. Most interesting is the connection between the sound of bamboo grass, which is onomatopoetically represented in the word itself (*sasa*) and the image of a sad retreat in the silence of dawn. Further, *nuru* is a variant form of the word for "to sleep" in addition to meaning "to become wet."

The first line of the woman's response, *mirumenaki,* means "not in a presentable condition"; the metaphor in the English comes from the included word *mirume,* which is a kind of seaweed. "Cove," *ura,* also means "hatred," and *karu* both "to go away" and "to reap" (the latter applies to the action of gathering seaweed). A possible variant reading overlooked by Japanese scholars—possible in that calligraphic manuscripts make no provisions for marking word boundaries—would be to read the last line (*ashi tayuku kuru*) as "you will return tomorrow" (*ashita yuku kuru*).* This gives the feeling of the tides which bring the seaweed in as well as the idea of the vicissitudes of life which bring a lover or take him away.

In this episode we must deal with the adjective *irogonomi-naru*. Applied to a man it is often translated as "lusty"; this is fine provided that we understand it in terms of the roving ways of an Arthurian character. When a woman is labeled *irogonomi,* however, the usual translation is "licentious" or "promiscuous." This is wholly unacceptable as it is more fitting of the word's meaning during the Tokugawa period (1600–1868). To Heian society an *irogonomi* woman was one well versed not only in the physical pleasures and techniques of love but in the social customs—like poetry—

---

* While this is a potential variant, it would only be received through *visual* contact with the poem because the sequence *yuku kuru* is stretching grammar beyond reasonable limits in spoken form. Thus, a chance reading might produce the variant, but this would not be acceptable as an utterable line of poetry.

surrounding them; more important, she was fully aware of all the problems entailed by a sexually oriented intrigue. Thus, rather than a damnable quality, I find *irogonomi* a mark of social achievement which could well be lauded.

DAN XXVI: Commentators on this episode have deliberately misinterpreted the grammatical structure of the prose in order to use the Fifth Ward as an indicator of the Narihira-Takako affair (see above, V), but the original letter of complaint is from the hero's friend and *not* the hero.

Looking at the poem, we should note that its tone and the details of its imagery (e.g., the foreign—Chinese—vessel) are not characteristic of standard Japanese *uta*. Since the poem was part of a man-to-man exchange, it is quite possible that the original poem was in Chinese, which was more commonly used by men; this would explain the intrinsic "difference" we may feel. Because the tale as a whole was directed toward an audience which could not read Chinese, the hypothesized Chinese original has been either translated or paraphrased. There are other examples of this elsewhere in *Ise,* and the Japanese *uta* provided are frequently of poor quality. I think we may assume with a fair degree of certainty that such poor *uta* are the result of noncorrespondence between the structures, imagery, and tone of the Chinese *shih* and the Japanese form.

DAN XXVII: In the original, "quarters" is *moto.* This word appears with high frequency in *Ise* and is translated according to my own sense of the context as quarters, house, room, mansion, etc. Here the choice is dependent upon the hero's being geographically situated so that he could possibly overhear her poem; thus "quarters" would mean her rooms at the palace where they both served.

This episode does not make a great deal of sense and it is likely that some of the connective prose has been lost. The two poems have very little to do with each other, making the whole seem rather bizarre if not wholly enigmatic.

A note with respect to the character of this woman: her comportment is acceptable, but she remains strange. If she were more fully drawn, I have the feeling she would quite resemble Hanachirusato (the Lady from the Village of Falling Flowers) in *Genji*.

DAN XXVIII: This poem contains a complex play on *augo katami ni*, meaning both "difficult to get to see each other" and a beam and the water buckets attached to each end; as is evident, I have found no way to capture this in English. The use of "vessel" in the translation lacks the power to evoke such an image, but it is the only word suited to both the prosodic and lexical demands of the poem.

This woman is another who is referred to as *irogonomi*, here translated as "flirtatious"; for a fuller explanation, see above, XXV.

DAN XXIX: The "Flower Celebration" was a birthday celebration held in conjunction with the cherry blossoms on the fortieth birthday and every successive decade. A detailed depiction of this may be found in *Genji*, "*Momiji no Ga*" (Festival of Red Leaves)—though this shows the same festivities held at the time of the turning of the autumn leaves.

In order to understand the emotions of the poem *per se,* it may be helpful to rely on historical fact. The heir apparent would have been Prince Jōmei, son of Emperor Seiwa and Takako, who had become his empress. The celebration would probably have been in honor of her father, Fujiwara no Nagara. Needless to say, a meeting between Narihira and Takako under such circumstances would be extremely painful, even though they would not have met face to face.

DAN XXX: *Tama no o* (see above, XIV) is translated literally in the poem though it functions as a *makurakotoba;* the last line (*nagaku miyuran*) is translated somewhat freely in order to catch the lightness with which the hero takes her rebuff. In the original there is also the contrast of long (*nagaku*) and short (in the *makurakotoba*)—paralleled by tall and short in English; he is thus saying that her heart grows more and more bitter.

This woman is presented as bitter and hard-hearted, but much of this we may assume to be self-exonerating exaggeration on the part of the hero, who after all would have had to be the active agent in the prolongation of the affair.

DAN XXXI: The two lines quoted are allegedly taken from a poem in the *Zokumanyōshū* according to the commentary of Sanjōnishi Sanetaka (1455–1537), *Isemonogatari Chokkai.* The whole of this poem runs as follows:

> *wasureyuku*
> *tsurasa wa ikani*
> *inochi araba*

yoshi ya kusayo yo
naran sa ga mimu

Gone and forgotten
bitternesses somehow still
have a breath of life:
I foresee this blade of grass
anon shall wither away.

The woman in this episode may be the same one who
appeared in XIX, but the setting is one in which she feels
more brave. Here, among her companions, there is no
reluctance to come out with a rather biting allusion.

DAN XXXII: This poem contains the most overtly sexual
image we have seen so far. More than the evident physical
conjunction of woof and warp is suggested: this is damask
brocade, and the "colors"—in the fullest sense as detailed
earlier—are constantly changing to form an elaborately
variegated pattern.

DAN XXXIII: The woman's poem uses *funasasu sao,* "a
staff used for poling a small boat," as an *engo* for *sashite,* "to
indicate" (also, to pole a boat). In the English I have adjusted
the imagery of both poems in order to achieve the visual
effect of the scene as a whole.

The locale of this episode is not far from the modern
Ashiya City, removed enough from Kyoto that we can
accept this as having been a truly provincial area where
inakabi would be expected. She seems well aware of the

伊勢物語

unlikelihood of the hero's making frequent trips to her, but the author's comment in the last line indicates that the geographical placement of this woman could be an intrinsic flaw, to the mind of the most privileged society.

DAN XXXIV: The exaggerated tone of the translation of the poem is a reflection not only of the quality of the original but also my personal affirmative response to the author's comment at the end. Such overreaction was typical of the Heian court gentleman, so vividly exemplified by the hero of *Ise* (though not necessarily Narihira himself) and, later, Prince Genji.

DAN XXXV: Where the poem in XXXII was what I would term overtly sexual in its imagery, this poem is openly erotic both in image and intent as well. There is a clear *ruika* (source poem) in the *Manyōshū* (no. 763) by Ki no Omina Oshishi:

> *tama no o*
> *awao ni yorite*
> *musubereba*
> *arite nochi ni mo*
> *awazarame ya mo*

> Like a silken string
> twined into a hollow cord
> bound in harmony—
> Though our years are much increased
> shall we no more meet in love?

The reply to this by Ōtomo no Yakamochi, one of the anthology's chief editors, is as follows:

> *momo tose ni*
> *oijita idete*
> *yoyomu tomo*
> *ware wa itowaji*
> *koi wa masu tomo*

> In my hundredth year
> when my teeth have fallen out
> and my back is bent—
> Never will you be too old
> for my ever constant love.

We must look at our poem in the light of this earlier exchange. While Lady Ki's and Yakamochi's poems express a primarily emotional love, Lady Ki uses the verb *musubu,* "to tie, twine"; by the time of *Ise* this verb had come to signify a sexual liaison. Understood in this context and noticing the change of the last two lines, there seems little doubt about the hero's motives. Moreover, both he and the woman would automatically be mindful of the original in the *Manyōshū* and even more so of the response.

DAN XXXVI: The only interesting point here is the character of the woman: she is either coy enough or experienced enough (the two are by no means mutually exclusive) to formulate her complaint as a most indirect question.

DAN XXXVII: For "well experienced in love" (iro-gonomi-naru) see above, XXV. As we are told the hero is "uneasy" we may suppose that the woman is irogonomi to the point of being capable of infidelity. In his poem the hero compares her to the morning-glory, a flower which fades before the evening (and his coming). Her response makes the sash of her gown the symbol of her fidelity. Of course, her poem specifies that both should be faithful; since male constancy was not much expected at this period it is possible that she is, on the contrary, admitting her own fickleness by emphasis on the hero's responsibilities to her.

DAN XXXVIII: Aritsune first appeared in XVI, but I would like to suggest that chronologically this episode is earlier in the historical sense. I do not get any sense of the personal disgrace into which he had fallen in XVI, and for that reason I have translated gari (synonymous with moto, see above, XXVII) as "estate."

In considering the structure of the entire tale, it seems to me that Aritsune's appearances may be of great significance. He appears first in XVI signaling the end of the hero's earliest exploits. (As the historical Narihira's father-in-law, he may also be some sort of "father image" in the tale.) He appears in this episode, and this appearance seems to coincide with the end of a second period in the hero's life, as well as marking the beginning of his political ascendancy (or, at least, the tale's concern with his political career). His next appearance is in LXXXVII, which concerns Prince Koretaka. Narihira's support of this prince over his younger half-brother who later ascended the throne brought on the decline of his political fortunes. The fact that Aritsune does not appear in the textual sequence leading to LXIX (the hero's affair with the Ise Priestess), rather than negating the value of these observations (which after all are tentative), shows a dualism in the structure. That is, the affair with the Priestess formed the beginning of one early series of texts (the *Koshikibu Naishi-bon,* of which only fragments are now extant), and it would appear that the author treated this sequence both as separate from the cyclical rise and fall of the hero and as a segment to be integrated within the whole framework of life—attaining manhood in Dan I—and death (in CXXV).

The two poems in this episode are a much clearer example of the problem discussed above in XXVI, namely, hypothetical conversions from original Chinese *shih.* In the original Japanese these two poems lack even the lyric nature of the poem in XXVI; they are uninteresting, somewhat unintelligible, and almost thoroughly unpoetic. In fact, the quality of these poems is so poor that we may assume with much more security than in the earlier case that the original exchange was written in Chinese.

DAN XXXIX: The emperor referred to is Emperor Junna (r. 823–33), the third son of Emperor Kammu; the title used comes from the location of an auxiliary palace. His daughter, Princess Takaiko, died on the fifteenth day of the fifth month, 848, at the age of nineteen.

The other historical figures mentioned are Minamoto no Itaru, grandson of Emperor Saga, and his grandson, Minamoto no Shitagau. Shitagau (911–83) was a well-known poet and scholar. He helped edit the *Gosenshū,* interpreted linguistic problems of the *Manyōshū,* and compiled the

Wamyōruijushō, the first Sino-Japanese dictionary. The picture that the episode gives us of Itaru is not to be taken at face value; rather, this is probably a parody of the historical figure for the author's fictional purposes (or for some similar reason which we can no longer hope to discover). Moreover, the editorial "retraction" of this made in the interpolation may be interpreted as a deference to Shitagau, a contemporary of Ise's unknown author, and to that family's own royal lineage.

The cultural content of this episode may well perplex the Western reader. A funeral, especially within the Imperial family, was first and foremost a Court ceremony. As with all other official ceremonies, the color and pomp were so splendid that all the ladies of the upper aristocracy were eager not only to attend but to vie with one another for the best view. The hero joins the party of ladies not for any amorous purposes but to view the ceremony without actually being seen himself. The "critical eyes" to which the ladies fear the fireflies' light may expose them are not Itaru's—as the carriage blinds were drawn—but the hero's.

The reference in the poems to the extinguishing of a flame is an allusion to a passage in the *Lotus Sutra (Hokkekyō)* describing the entrance of the Buddha into Nirvana. The frame of reference adopted in the translation, however, is that of the winds of Fate. Itaru's poem may be variously interpreted: the emphatic quality of the last line could show a lack of propriety and some disrespect toward the late princess, or he could be implying that she has gone not to death but—like the Buddha—to a better life.

DAN XL: This episode easily lends itself to comparison

with the story of Kashiwagi's death in the *Tale of Genji*. (Ikeda sees more of a comparison with Murasaki no Ue's illness in *Wakana-ge*, "Young Shoots II," but I feel this is more dependent on lexical usage than on overall structure.) The detail with which this episode is structured and developed is, in my opinion, almost equal to those techniques found in *Genji*.

The author, in this episode, specifies the hero as *wakaki otoko*, which I have translated as "a very young and inexperienced man." Because of etymological and traditional semantic interpretations, I have usually translated *otoko* as "young man" in contrast to its modern general meaning of male. Its modification by *wakaki*, "young," necessitated the extended phrase in English, for whereas *otoko* by itself covers an age range of twelve to twenty, here with the modification the quality of youth is merely coupled with inexperience.

DAN XLI: The end of the twelfth month was the time of preparation for the celebration of the New Year at the court. The garment would need reblocking because the Japanese kimono is taken apart for washing and then resewn. The cloak sent by the brother-in-law was green in color, indicating the sixth—and lowest—rank of the court officialdom. Each rank had prescribed colors based on the adopted Chinese bureaucratic system.

The poem's meaning may be paraphrased as follows: just as from a distance not even the keenest eyesight could distinguish the quality of the various dye-plants growing in the field, so I the wealthier man cannot morally distinguish between the duties to wife and sister-in-law.

伊勢物語

The interpolation postdates the *Kokinshū* (905) because its meaning is "this poem is the same as that poem which precedes it" in that anthology. Since the *Kokinshū* attributes this poem to Narihira, the poorer man would have been Fujiwara no Toshiyuki, husband of Aritsune's other daughter. In light of this, the whole episode may be seen in a political, anti-Fujiwara sense (the political failures of the Ki and Arihara clans were to the benefit of the Fujiwaras if not directly engineered by them).

DAN XLII: Here is another *irogonomi* woman (see above, XXV) already involved (we feel) with more than one man. The fact that the hero is still magnetically drawn to her might be a hint that she was a rather skillful sex partner. Unfortunately, we do not have her reactions to the hero's poem which might let us see deeper into her character. Further, what I have translated as "occupied with business matters" could have a different interpretation: due to the lack of clear phrasal relationships, the subject of *sawaru koto arite* could be the woman, in which case the meaning would probably be that she was menstruating and was thus taboo.

The last line of the poem in translation is designed to tie in with the vivid imagery of the original which picks out the faint footprints the hero has left on his last departure. Extended, this idea could be rather comical; that is, for another lover to use the same tracks without destroying them, he would have to walk backwards.

DAN XLIII: Prince Kaya (d. 871) was the seventh child of Emperor Kammu; his possession of royal blood, however, did not give him insuperable claims on any particular woman. The second gentleman must remain a mystery figure beyond our identification of him as a courtier. The third is our hero as it is he who writes the poems.

In the first poem there is the problem of "cuckoo" which only roughly corresponds to the original *hototogisu*. Needless to say, it is most infrequent that translations of names for flora and fauna will have a high level of correspondence; in this case the cuckoo is the closest bird, but there is a further problem: five syllables of Japanese into two syllables of English. The solution is to take the poetic sense of this bird's song as conceived by the Japanese (though in reality it is a rather hard and unpleasant song which the *hototogisu* provides). In the next poem, *shide no taosa* stands as a circumlocution for the name of the bird. According to legend (one with Chinese origins), this name arises from the fact that the cuckoo is the link between the world we inhabit and the Land of the Dead, flying across the boundary of "death's mountain" (*shide no yama*).

Both Ikeda and Ōtsu interpret the syllabic sequence *keshikiotorite* as *keshiki o torite*, "humoring him"; I have taken this as *keshiki otorite*, "her feelings hurt." The feeling of the preceding poem is not substantially different from many to which women in other episodes have taken offense. Thus, I find my syllabification to be more consistent with the entire tenor of the tale. While there is graphemic evidence in the manuscript contradictory to my interpretation, the copyist of the manuscript has in other places frequently made mistakes confusing *o*, *wo*, and *ho* (here we find *wo* while we should expect *o* for *otorite*).

DAN XLIV: The rites of farewell (*hanamuke*) consisted of a banquet after which the master of ceremonies, in this case the hero, took the reins of the horse on which the traveler was seated and led the horse out onto the road in the direction of the trip. The original is a simpler explanation in itself, for it literally means "nose pointing."

The garment given was a formal skirt (*mo*) worn usually by women. Travelers used these as early motorists used dusters; they hung down the back only (a sort of reverse apron) and kept the brocaded Court-cloak clean.

DAN XLV: The girl here is most typical of those found in later Heian fiction: she finds herself in love, cannot find the courage to speak because of her careful upbringing, becomes ill, and—this last is not obligatory—eventually dies.

The hero's seclusion was not wholly out of mourning and the sadness engendered by having discovered a potential love too late; the taboo from his contact with death obligated him to withdraw from active social intercourse for at least a few days. The "music of the liturgy" was played to soothe the soul of the departed. It seems to have been a combination of wind and string ensembles without much percussion. The hero, having been trained in the social arts, would have joined in on either the flute or zither (or both).

DAN XLVI: We are unable to discover anything about the identity or the character of this friend. His loneliness is natural, as life outside the capital city was so culturally deprived as to be considered worse than death by all those

of the aristocracy who faced the call of provincial govern-
mental service. The strength of emotion and the poetic
sensibility expressed in this friend's letter seem so outstanding as to demand the special typographical distinction
available for long quotes in English even though there is
no such demarcation in the manuscript.

DAN XLVII: My translations of these poems try to catch
the complex religious imagery of the originals while still
maintaining the humorous tone simultaneously implied.
Ōnusa are strips of white paper used in Shinto purification
ceremonies; they are rubbed on the body to transfer some
taboo or uncleanliness to the purity of the paper and then
cast into a river so that the evil is carried away to the sea.
Often they are arranged on a staff to resemble leaves; it is
in this form that the woman uses the word to symbolize
the hero who is sought after by so many women. The
response he makes is a light insult, for he bemoans the fact
that when he, as this strip of paper, comes finally to rest, it
is to a shallow (a woman who cares little for him) that he
must by fate drift.

DAN XLVIII: For an explanation of the rites of farewell
see above, XLIV.
   In the overall structure of the episode, the traveler who
failed to show up for his own farewell party seems to be a
fictional excuse to use this particular poem. The woman
who is waiting for the hero must be some recent acquisition
as the hero does not dare to keep her waiting very long.

DAN XLIX: The reader should not be tempted to interpret this episode in terms of an incestuous relationship. Marriages between half- brothers and sisters, while not overly common, were not strictly taboo. The author's use of a humble position for the hero in relation to the girl would indicate that her mother's status was above that of the hero's; thus an affair between them would become even more difficult. She feels no shock at the hero's interest in her, yet her innocence and naïveté seem a disguise learned at a rather early age—if it is true that she is having an affair with someone else. Her hint that she might be favorably inclined toward the hero at some later date indicates to me the author's somewhat stereotyped concept of Narihira's entire family.

The imagery of the poems depends upon the use of "young grass" (see above, XII) as a *makurakotoba* and the verb *musubu*, "to tie, weave" (see above, XXXV). While the full range of meaning can rise to the surface, that surface *per se* seems more properly viewed in the metaphor of nature.

DAN L: It seems rather evident to me that the "hate" felt on both sides of this poetic exchange is engendered by love. In comparison with the other women in the tale, this lady appears extremely bold—so much so that she may even be a prototype of the woman Sei Shōnagon finds to be herself in the *Pillow Book (Makura no Sōshi)*.

The image of piling eggs one on top of the other is taken from a didactic Chinese story of the Han period in which the "state" decays as the rulers thus amuse themselves. The dew as a symbol of evanescence in the second poem is readily understandable. In the third poem we are asked to imagine the impossible, thus receiving a third metaphor for human frailties; this poem, moreover, is almost a perfect duplication of a poem by the Chinese poet Li Po. There are various explanations of "writing numbers" on running water, the most general explaining the sequence as 1, 2, 3 for which the characters are respectively one, two, and three horizontal strokes. Even this is impossible, thus the tenor of the metaphor is again achieved.

The last poem is a summary of all these similes, ending in a warning—or lament—that there is nothing in this world which can escape the flow of time. While this could be interpreted as an expression of the Buddhistic sense of the transitory world (*mujōkan*), I see it merely as the early Heian view of nature in constant flux.

DAN LI: The "front garden" was a small informal garden located near the entrance to the house. The formal garden was architecturally conceived as a corporate part of the plan for the residence proper.

The chrysanthemum is a hardy plant known best in Japan for its autumn blossoms, but the hero signifies that the true love he bears lives on even after the flowers—its outward expressions—have withered. This episode's "someone" may once again be his great love, the lady central to the first dozen or so episodes of the tale.

DAN LII: The "festival delicacy" sent is specified as *chimaki*. The festival implied is Tango, or the Iris Festival, analogous to the Chinese Dragon Boat Festival, held on the fifth day of the fifth month. The *chimaki* was made of glutinous rice cakes with a hard crust wrapped, usually, in miscanthus reed, then tied with strings of five colors. From the content of the poem, it would appear that sweet flags (*ayame*) could be substituted as the wrapping. In the poem, *karu* is *kakekotoba* (see above, IX) meaning both "to cut" and "to hunt," and, extended, "to reap."

DAN LIII: It appears—with *Ise* and *Genji* as the main source books—that Heian gentlemen spent a good many nights in conversation of love. The lover must always leave before the tryst is discovered, and cock's crow usually means the rest of the house is starting to awaken. While our hero has been talking more than half the night, he still hasn't managed to tell the girl of his feelings for her (which, considering his roving proclivities, is probably just as well for her sake). His sincere façade of an almost burdened reluctance to leave led me to the pun in English between "told" and "tolled."

DAN LIV: In paraphrase the hero's meaning is as follows: I cannot visit in person because you do not wish to see me; all I can trust is that I will visit you in my dreams. (The Japanese believed that the soul literally went from the dreamer to the dream object in such a situation.) Even then as my heart (soul) flies through the heavens, my sleeve is soaked with dew just as in the real life of my misery tears flow in abundance.

DAN LV: The overstatement and emotional exaggeration of both this poem and the one preceding it are excellent examples of the self-indulging sentimentalism so typical of the Heian courtier. Oddly enough, we hardly ever find such hyperemotionalism in the poetry of their female contemporaries. After the fall of the aristocracy, retrospective explanation blamed the decline on the "effeminate" nature of the men who were running the government. Perhaps the Heian man would have done better to more accurately "feminize" himself, thus removing what most certainly was a repugnantly flabby emotionalism.

DAN LVI: While the sentiment of this poem, too, is exaggerated, the vivid scenery of the metaphor attracts us. His sleeve is the thatch roof of a hermit's cottage, catching the heavy dew where it stands wholly surrounded by the tall wild grasses.

DAN LVII: The measuring worm (*warekarami*) is said to live inside the hollow spores of certain seaweeds, cracking them open when it becomes a mature insect. I find this poem a rather unusual one in that it views love as an instrument of destruction, a view not often expressed by the Japanese of the classical period.

DAN LVIII: Earlier I have mentioned historical details in the lives of Arihara no Narihira and his contemporaries as possible clues to the understanding of various passages. Further, I have suggested that the author's purposeful symbolization of the hero should discourage us from dwelling on these facts of history. This warning is necessitated by the fact that all too often *Ise-monogatari* is viewed solely from its quasi-historical aspect. In order to fully understand

伊勢物語

any work of literature, it is often most helpful to consider the way in which it was received at the time of its composition.

This critical preparation may at first seem out of place as appended to this relatively nonunique episode, but there is more than ample reason for a detailed consideration here of the interpretation of the main character. After fifty-seven episodes in which the characterization of the hero is drawn wholly from context, here in the fifty-eighth we have a direct statement from the author: "a young man who was a ladies' man to the limits of his resourcefulness. . . ." Why?

Any attentive reader already knows that the hero is *irogonomi,* "a ladies' man"; why say it point blank? More puzzling is the premodifier *kokoro tsukite,* literally, "exhausting the heart." I can offer the following solution, but the reader must understand that this is only one solution, derived—in my case— from several years of constant work on this tale.

The Heian reader came to *Ise-monogatari* already well acquainted with the life and poetic work of Narihira. It is likely that he would wish to view the hero of this work as the historical figure rather than as a personification of certain aspects of that historical figure's character in symbolic form. Yet the author to this point never names his hero; nor does he create any narrative situation which could refer *only* to Narihira.

This episode takes place at Nagaoka, a small city not far from Heian, which served as the temporary capital from 784 to 794 while the new city was under construction. Commentators have for centuries explained the appearance in this episode of "ladies of the Imperial family" by reminding us that the many daughters of Emperor Kammu lived in Nagaoka. Why have they, then, overlooked the fact that Narihira's mother, Princess Ito, was also one of Kammu's daughters? The same commentators cannot understand why the hero's house is referred to as a palace (*miya*), explaining this word away as an error in copying. It is not. The house referred to belonged to Princess Ito. Yet, the text says the hero built it (*ie tsukurite*) which I submit means *tsukurinaoshite*, "put into good order and repair." How did I arrive at this interpretation?

Princess Ito died in 861 when Narihira was thirty-six. If we set the hero's age in the first episode at fifteen and accept Narihira's age of fifty-five at his death for the last episode, the tale covers forty years. This episode is near the midpoint of the tale, thus making the hero about thirty-five. The geographical setting of Nagaoka combined with all the hints at Narihira to this point in the tale would certainly have fully prepared the Heian reader to understand without any hesitation "Narihira" when reading "young man." But if he were in Nagaoka and his mother were living, we would expect her to appear, which she does not. Further, whether she was alive or not there would be no need for Narihira to build a house, as hers would be available to him. Imagining myself a Heian reader, the only conclusion which I could draw from the network of confused and contradictory facts would be that Princess Ito is dead, and Narihira as a faithful son (a quality we but rarely see in the hero) is keeping her former palace in respectable shape.

With this understanding of the contradictory play between what the prose actually says and what the Heian reader was prepared to have it say, we can understand the author's one and only direct, adjectival characterization of the hero. The Heian reader had so much evidence that this hero actually *was* Narihira that the author needed to conclusively define that hero as *not*-Narihira, as Narihira's *irogonomi* singled out, magnified, and symbolized for all time.

DAN LIX: The exaggeration mentioned above (LV, LVI) is also operant in this episode, but to a degree which I find extremely comical: the first thing the hero does upon "reviving" is to recite a poem thanking "the gods" for saving him.

DAN LX: The Receiving Officer (*shizō*) was a provincial official whose duty it was to take care of lodging, meals, etc., for any Imperial or Court delegate passing through his province.

It was the duty of Court-appointed delegates to carry Imperial messages regarding official actions or any change in the state of affairs of the country to the Usa Shrine, located in the modern Ōita Prefecture. Enshrined at Usa were Emperor Ōjin (r. 270?–310?); his mother, Empress Jingū (Regent, 201?–69?); and the Buddhist deity Hachiman, god of war. According to traditional history, it was during Ōjin's reign that writing, sericulture, weaving, dyeing, and Confucian learning were introduced to Japan by Wani and other Korean immigrants from the state of Kudara. Thus Ōjin and the other deities at Usa were regarded so highly that the state of the country's welfare was periodically reported to them.

DAN LXI: Tsukushi is the premodern name for the island of Kyūshū. It is at such a distance from Heian that it is synonymous with the severest degree of *hinabi* (see above, XIV).

Somekawa (River of the Dye) is in Fukuoka Prefecture, and Tawarejima (Island of Deceit) is in neighboring Kumamoto Prefecture. The woman's poem employs a rather stock metaphor on *iro* (see above, XX) which is much less *hinabi* than we would expect. The hero's reply is loosely structured, showing through mediocre poetry his lack of interest in her. The mixed metaphor of the translation of his poem attempts to catch this loose structure. The idea of "salt and pepper" is thus stretched between the first and last lines, with "peppery" used as a semantic pun.

DAN LXII: In the second poem, "Meeting Province" is a translation of Ōmi (or *au-mi,* "meet and see") Province.

This lady is uncultured and lacking in common sense, though she is to be preferred to the provincial of episode XIV. She trusts one man to take care of her after she has forsaken the hero but winds up in the retinue of a third in the provinces. (The lady in episode LX at least got herself a provincial officer of the Court.) She fails to recognize the hero; then she is at a loss for words (or an *uta* in practice), an unforgivable crime even for the early Heian period. Her excuse is almost incoherent, and she never does manage a poem. Lastly, she discards his cloak, which probably would have been her only valuable piece of property in her flight. She does not even have the propriety to renounce the world as the lady in LX did.

DAN LXIII: Dreams were believed to portend the future; thus her false dream was consciously constructed so as to facilitate the answer given her by the third son.

Colonel Zaigo means Narihira; *zai* is the Sinic pronunciation of the *ari* in Arihara, and *go* means the fifth (son). Since the clan title of Arihara was first conferred upon Prince Abo's sons and Narihira was the fifth, there can be no question that the author is giving us a name. Not *the* name, but *a* name. The appearance of Narihira's Court-title name does not wholly contradict the discussion of episode LVIII; in fact it may strengthen it. Many historical figures contemporary to Narihira are named—for example Aritsune, Itaru, and later Koretaka, Yukihira, and others—why not Narihira himself? Does the fact that Colonel Zaigo appears automatically imply that he is the hero? I think not. It is possible that the "third son"—of whom nothing concrete is said—is the hero in this episode and that he is "learning" from the model concretely exhibited in the person of Narihira. This would follow with my idea (see above, XLIX) that the author has extended *irogonomi* as a symbol to the hero's entire family (here, the mother). There is no concrete evidence in the text either to support or negate this idea; but as a critical suggestion it is not outside the realm of possibility.

In another aspect, the appearance of one of Narihira's names is an important clue to the composition of the tale. It shows us the existence of some form of poetic diary written by Narihira himself (referring to oneself in the third person was a very common practice) which became the major source for the author. It is at this point we should distinguish poet, author(s), and compiler. Usually the poet is Narihira. The compiler is that person who added the historical interpolations and may have had a hand in the final arrangement of the sequence of the episodes. The author—or authors, no one can say which—transformed Narihira's diary into a tale (*monogatari,* in the Heian sense), made the hero a symbolic figure embodying *miyabi* and *irogonomi* (see above, I and XXV respectively), and ordered the episodes. Perhaps an author-A devised the sequence of the *Koshikibu Naishi-bon* (see above, XXXVIII) and an author-B rearranged them in the sequence we have today.

DAN LXIV: The use of "incredulous" for *izuku narikemu* is meant in the sense that the hero was hard put to believe that with all of his social skills he could not find out more about this woman. Clearly, this woman has no desire to become involved with the hero; the haughty attitude of her poem might suggest a rather skillful disguise of the spinster type when in fact she probably was already involved with enough men to keep her busy.

DAN LXV: Notes to this episode fall naturally into three groups. The first of these includes the following random explanations of life within the grounds of the Imperial Palace.

Women were forbidden to wear either vermilion or purple except by special Imperial order; here I have interpolated vermilion rather than purple as the woman is not yet in a position where it is clear that she is to be raised to the position of Empress. The Great Hall, or Seiryōden, is the building in which the Emperor passed most of the day. It is just west of the central building (Shishinden) of the

伊
勢
物
語

Imperial Palace. The "dais" was one of the larger rooms of the Seiryōden, used as a common gathering place for the Imperial concubines and their individual entourages. In addition to the quarters each concubine maintained within the Palace, she had a residence in the city, called her *sato,* to which she might return for vacations, confinement during pregnancy, etc. The Groundskeepers (*tonomozukasa*), in addition to supervising the maintenance of the Palace, served as gatesmen, lamplighters, etc.; lesser nobles rather than commoners filled these positions. The reason for the hero's removal of his boots is that no shoes were permitted in any of the main buildings of the palace.

The second group of points deals with religious practice. The word "practice" should be stressed and differentiated from "belief." The society of this period enjoyed the color and ornamental ceremony of both Shinto and Esoteric Buddhism, but they rarely gave serious consideration to the metaphysical implications of their conglomerate religion. The "diviners" followed the rituals of the Yin-Yang theory prescribed in the *Classic of Change* (*I Ching*). The Shinto liturgists, either male or female, performed the native rites of purification; these rites, not too dissimilar from the classical Greek libations, were carried out on a riverbank (see the notes on *ōnusa,* XLVII). The "Saving Name" which the Emperor chanted was the recitation of the name of salvation of the Amida Buddha, a practice central to the Pure Land (Jōdō) Sect.

The third point of consideration is the historical and literary relevance of this episode. The hero is identified as a member of the Arihara clan, but not necessarily Narihira. In the historical interpolation, Mizu-no-O was Emperor

Seiwa (r. 858–76); if this episode's hero is to be Narihira, either the fictional age of the hero is wrong (Narihira having been eighteen years older than Takako) or the emperor would have been Emperor Montoku (r. 850–58) in which case there would arise a confusion between Dowager Empress Akiko (for Seiwa, the Lady of the Fifth Ward) and Nobuko, Montoku's mother. The lady here is the highest of nobility, cousin to the Dowager and almost betrothed to the Emperor. Her vital concern over her position at the Court is explicitly mentioned, but the author's sentiment leaves us with the feeling that as a woman she is just too weak to resist the hero's love. The whole story, especially the reaction of the Emperor and the Dowager, is so fully developed a piece of fiction that this episode must have been the model for Murasaki's subplot dealing with Prince Genji's affair with Lady Oborozukiyo and the subsequent exile to Suma arranged by the Dowager Kokiden.

DAN LXVI: The possession of clan estates outside of the capital here refers to a different locale than that mentioned in the first episode. It is never clear whether these lands are general properties of the clan or personal holdings. Land was the basis for political power, and the areas specified are not such places as to indicate any major power.

DAN LXVII: This episode can well be compared to XXIII as they take place in the same location. The influence of seasonal conditions on the aesthetic sense of the poetry is most interesting. Here the wide, white expanse creates a very cold sadness, whereas the clouded night sky and brewing autumn storm of XXIII induce a heavy melancholy. What seems a direct relation between season and poetic temperament is an important aspect of Japanese poetry, especially that in the *uta* form.

DAN LXVIII: The statement of the geographical location seems almost farcical, but it is intended to emphasize the literal meaning of *sumiyoshi*—"good living." In the original, this repetition is rather powerful: *sumiyoshi no kōri, sumiyoshi no sato, sumiyoshi no hama*.

DAN LXIX: While episode LXV is the longest of the *monogatari*, there can be no doubt that this episode is in many ways the most important and best piece of writing that *Ise* has to offer. In order to deal most effectively with the episode as a whole, a discussion of points of cultural interest will be kept to a minimum.

The Imperial Falconer was officially appointed to supervise the hunt for game to be served at the Imperial tables. More important, perhaps, was his unofficial job of inspecting the state of provincial government; this certainly is the explanation for the most obsequious—though unwanted—treatment he receives from the Court's appointed governor. The High Priestess at the Great Ise Shrine (the principal shrine of the sun goddess Amaterasu, matriarchal forebear to the Imperial line) was an unmarried and customarily virginal Imperial Princess appointed upon the accession of a new emperor. The tradition was carried on as a fairly standardized practice from the reign of the semihistorical Emperor Sujin through the rule of Emperor Go-Daigo (r. 1318–39). Even by the time of Montoku, however, the position of the priestess was regarded quite leniently—though the need for secrecy in such affairs was immensely greater than that maintained in general circles.

Because this episode appears in the first position of the *Koshikibu Naishi-bon* (also called the *Kari no Tsukai,* "Imperial Falconer," series of texts), we must give special consideration to its structure and literary implications. From the viewpoint of structure this episode shows the acme of artistry in *Ise;* the prose flows into poetry with complete naturalness. This places the *uta* form precisely where it should be in the context of the literary history of the Heian period; that is, the *uta*—or poetry—was the profound depth of human emotion transformed into speech. In Japan—and this is probably a universal—poetry is the organic basis of vocal behavior. The Japanese have maintained this psychophysical attitude toward poetry to the present day; within ordinary conversation it is most natural to express deep emotion in poetry: *as a part of the flow of speech.* On a broad scale this attitude is more functionally embodied in the *Tale of Genji,* but its appearance here should be sufficient proof of the level of development of native Japanese literature in the mid-tenth century.

Prior to the appearance of *Genji (ca.* 1008) the only works of fiction now extant are *Ise* and *Taketori-monogatari (The Tale of the Old Bamboo Cutter).* We know the titles of others now irretrievably lost from remarks in *Genji,* Murasaki's diary, and the diary of Izumi Shikibu, but literary historians are hard put either to posit the quality of these works or to explain the appearance of *Genji,* which is unquestionably the finest piece of fiction in all of classical Japanese literature, only half a century after *Ise.* The intervening works (such as *Ochikubo-monogatari, Utsubo-monogatari, Yamato-mono-gatari, Tōnomine Shōshō-monogatari,* etc.) are of varying quality both among themselves as representatives of the *monogatari* genre and internally as individual works.

A second major point of interest in this episode, therefore, is its importance in showing us that Narihira's diary was not nearly as developed as the *Kari no Tsukai* texts, and that he was not a writer of Japanese prose. If we compare the prose of this episode to the prose preface (*kotobagaki*) of the same poems in the *Kokinshū* (905), and if we add to this the criticism of Narihira by Ki no Tsurayuki, the editor of that anthology ("his emotions are excessive and his words lacking"—a subjugation of form to content), this becomes clear. It is my opinion that had Narihira been the master of a prose style equal to that found in this episode, he should have produced a fictional work of great magnitude which would have his name securely attached to it, and that such a work would not have been entirely lost to the history of Japanese literature. My conclusions, then, must be that *Ise* as a *monogatari* was written in the manner theorized by Dr. Fukui Teisuke in his article "The Transformation of Narihira's Private Collection into a Monogatari" [*Narihira Kashu no Monogatari-ka*], *Kokugo to Kokubungaku*, January 1954. Oversimplified, this theory suggests the existence of two authors who performed the transformations described in the notes to episode LXIII. I personally have another name to add to the list of persons who may have been the major author of this work, but that suggestion will be found in the notes to episode CVII.

DAN LXX: The location of the Ōyodo Ferry was either

in the same provincial district as the Great Ise Shrine (Ise Jingū) or a neighboring district. This episode and the three following it, together with LXIX, make the clearest example in *Ise* of sequentially ordered and related episodes. To a lesser degree this is true of episodes VII–XV, called the "Eastern Travel" (*Azuma-kudari*) sequence by Japanese scholars. Here, however, the sequence is good evidence of the incorporation of the *Koshikibu Naishi-bon* into this later structural organization of the text (see above, XXXVIII).

DAN LXXI: This episode presents an entirely different aspect of the events of LXIX. Apparently the hero essayed some kind of affair with one of the Priestess's maids prior to the night of her own visit to his rooms. In the poems, "Soul tempestuous" is my translation of *chihayaburu,* a *makurakotoba* for "deity, god" (*kami*). The "fence" is one of straw rope, surrounding any sacred spot. The second line of the hero's poem gains its jocularity from the emphatic usage of *-kashi* in the original.

DAN LXXII: There seems to be a definite relation between the poem here and the poem in episode LXX; clearly the woman (whom we may identify with the Priestess) has been informed that the hero is taking the ferry at Ōyodo. In her poem we find the standard pun on *matsu*: "to wait" and "pine tree" as well as the metaphorical idea of mountains and clouds (see above, XIX) changed to the pines (stationary) and waves (free).

DAN LXXIII: The hero's inability to communicate his feelings even by letter is easily understood if we identify this woman, as well, as the Priestess. The "laurel tree" in the moon is in a Chinese legend telling of a laurel of almost 1,000 feet which is metaphorically used to signify the moon's shadow, the dark cast of the crescent moon (a thing visible but nonconcrete).

DAN LXXIV: In the original of the poem, *koiwataru* gives the sense of sending one's love to someone fruitlessly, so that the longer she continues to reject him the less he is inclined to sustain his love. This led me to the doubled image of mountain/mount of rejection so high that love can no longer breathe.

DAN LXXV: The mention of Ōyodo in the first poem should not remind us of the Priestess; its use here is merely as a famous place of beauty in Ise Province. The use of waves, tears, salt and fresh water in all of these poems taken together shows an extended poetic exchange based on but a few words.

DAN LXXVI: While the "Consort" need not necessarily be Fujiwara no Takako, it is clear that this powerful clan is meant. The Ōhara Shrine is dedicated to their clan deity, Amenokoyane-no-mikoto, and almost all the Heirs Apparent after Emperor Kammu were children of Fujiwara mothers.

In this episode the hero is called an "old man" (*okina*) for the first time; this term would signify someone over the age of forty. Its use here signals the beginning of a long segment of the *monogatari* in which historical figures contemporary with Narihira figure prominently in the "plot."

The reward (*roku*) he receives from the Consort may have been some ornament or article of clothing. Distribution of such gifts is richly described throughout *Genji*. The hero receives one in his role as an Inner Palace Guard (a member of the *Konoezukasa*); taking Narihira and Takako as background models, this would create a most tender if not pathetic moment shortly before her elevation to the position of Empress in 875.

DAN LXXVII: The Tamura Emperor was Emperor Montoku (see above, LXV); his concubine Takakiko was the daughter of Fujiwara no Yoshiharu (she is not to be confused with Takako; see above, III and *passim*). Fujiwara no Tsuneyuki was not a particularly notable member of this clan, but the political implications here and in the next episode are clear: The Arihara clan is now coming under the same sort of attack used to reduce the power of the Ki clan (implied in XVI). References to various historical figures (beginning with Aritsune in XVI) make it clear that there is an allegorical political background to this tale centering on the Ki and Arihara clans. It is most fitting, therefore, that Narihira appears most often as Captain of the Right of the Imperial Stables (*Miginomumanokami*) rather than as Zaigo Chūjō (see above, LXIII), for the former post he occupied most of his political life. The author wishes to divert our attention from politics, however, as he makes it clear that, no matter how great the need to stifle Narihira as a politician, the hero is first and foremost a poet of incomparable stature.

DAN LXXVIII: The author's deliberate confusion of historical facts in creating a chronologically impossible situation is interesting to note. Prince Yamashina (his name after taking vows; otherwise Prince Saneyasu) was the fourth son of Emperor Nimmyō (r. 833–50); he became a monk in 859. Takakiko died in 858, a year before Yamashina had retreated from the world. Further, Tsuneyuki did not become General of the Right (*Utaishō*) until 866, and Narihira assumed his post in 865. This is all part of a device aimed at separating the hero from Narihira.

The "forty-ninth day" recitations of the Sutras were the last Buddhist masses read to save the soul of the departed and ended the seven-week period of religious mourning.

The description of the inscribing of the hero's poem on the rock by cutting away the moss so that the calligraphy showed on the smooth, glassy surface is probably the best example in *Ise* of the spirit of *miyabi* (see above, I) carried into action.

DAN LXXIX: According to the historical interpolation, the "clan" was the Arihara. Narihira is referred to as the Colonel (see above, LXIII and LXXVII). Yukihira (818–93), the Minister of the Center (*Chūnagon*), was Narihira's older brother. The poem's expression of political hopes is clear: an Imperial Prince related to us cannot but improve our fortunes.

DAN LXXX: The house mentioned is the hero's own residence referred to in self-deprecatory terms. Wistaria has a definite meaning: in Japanese it is *fuji,* the first character in Fujiwara. Like this clan's firm position in the political world, the wistaria is an extremely hardy vine which is not only difficult to get rid of but also often chokes the host around which it grows.

DAN LXXXI: We may learn from the location of the mansion that this Minister of the Left (*Hidari no Ōimōchi-gimi*) was Minamoto no Tōru (823–95). The Kamo River along with the Kasuga River forms a natural border within which the city of Heian was contained. For a description of fading chrysanthemums, see the notes to episode XVIII.

The use of *okina* (see above, LXXVI) is here qualified with *kata-i*, literally "to the side of the road"; this being the proper place of a beggar, its use here is self-deprecatory (allowing that the author injects himself into the hero he is creating).

Where the text gives *taishiki*, "dais," commentators correct this to *itashiki* (a metathesis of two syllables), "slat floor." While *taishiki* is not a standard word, I submit that the metathesis is unacceptable because the hero could not hobble over and stand *beneath* the slat floor.

DAN LXXXII: Next to Fujiwara no Takako, Prince Koretaka was the most important person in Narihira's life. As the first son of Emperor Montoku, he should rightfully have become emperor, but his mother was not a Fujiwara. She was the daughter of Ki no Natora, Lady Shizuko, Aritsune's sister. He was Heir Apparent for a while, but he was passed over in favor of his younger half-brother, Prince Korebito. Korebito was the son of Lady Akiko whose father Fujiwara no Yoshifusa (804–72) was the first of that clan to assume the title of Regent (*Sesshō*)—a position formerly restricted to members of the Imperial family. It was Narihira's support of Koretaka over Korebito (based on family alliances, see also above, XVI) that brought his political downfall.

As mentioned above (LXXVII), the Captain of the Right usually is associated with Narihira. The author is faced with another example of overwhelming evidence with the appearance of Koretaka (even more concrete than in LVIII) which he handles in a unique way: the parenthetical statement in which the author cannot remember the name of the hero. While this seems an obvious and poor device to us, I believe it was strong enough at the time to fool the ordinary Heian reader.

In the third and fourth poems, the legend on which the poets rely is that of the Weaving Star Vega who meets her lover, the Herdsman Star Altair (in the constellation Aquila), only once a year. This meeting is the basis of the Tanabata Festival, held on the seventh day of the seventh lunar month. (This contrasts with the "eleventh-night moon" of the prose, a phrase which seems to have no particular significance other than indicating the moon shortly before the night of the full moon.)

The hidden meanings of the last two poems are that the Ki clan is being completely eclipsed by the Fujiwaras with the failure of Koretaka (Aritsune's nephew) to win out over Korebito. Aritsune recites his two poems on behalf of the Prince; this was not an unusual practice. For example, the poem inscribed on the rock in episode LXXVIII, though composed by the hero, was offered as that of his superior, Tsuneyuki.

DAN LXXXIII: This episode is probably the one story in

all of *Ise* which most touches the Japanese sentiment. After the Prince's traditional "end-of-spring" hunt, the hero laments the shortness of the nights, thus giving us an early example of the Japanese preference for the autumn. The summer and autumn pass unmentioned, and in the winter Koretaka becomes a Buddhist monk. His withdrawal from society was prompted by the birth of the future Emperor Yōzei to Emperor Seiwa (Prince Korebito; see above, LXXXII) and Empress Takako. The picture of the two spending the night in Koretaka's lonely retreat with winter raging outside is extremely moving. The Prince could not but think of his younger brother's usurpation of his birthright, while Narihira dutifully commiserated. He had himself not only lost his political maneuverability in that affair, but the birth of Yōzei (Prince Jōmei, or Sada-aki) would certainly remind him of his affair with—if not lingering love for—Takako.

DAN LXXXIV: In the notes to episode XXXVIII, I suggested that that episode could chronologically precede XVI. Similarly, this episode refers to a point preceding episode LVIII. Narihira was Princess Ito's only child, Yukihira's mother having been another of Prince Abo's wives. While his emotion for his mother is exaggerated slightly, the picture of the hero here serves to reinforce that aspect of his character hinted at in LVIII.

DAN LXXXV: The Prince is Koretaka; we know this from the discussion of the fact that he has taken the vows of a certain order. Nevertheless, the chronology is false as Narihira was twenty years his senior. The mistake is delib-

伊勢物語

erate on two counts: First, it distinguishes again the hero and his Prince from the real figures. Second, it shows Narihira's humble devotion to Koretaka.

DAN LXXXVI: Here, again, the author describes the hero as *wakaki otoko* (see above, XL) to which he adds the pre-qualifier *ito*, "very." The girl is described as simply *wakaki onna*. I have translated them both as "very young" (omitting the "inexperienced" as it seems naturally implied). Women were expected to reach social maturity earlier, so the terms seem to balance out.

DAN LXXXVII: The poem which the author presents at the beginning is no. 278 in the *Manyōshū;* it explains the name Ashiya—*ashi*, "reed," and *ya*, "dwelling." The phrase "rough sea" (*nada;* also "open sea") comes from the second line of the original Japanese (*nada no shioyaki*).

The description of the Nunobiki Falls (cf. the sentence describing Mt. Fuji after the third poem in episode IX), with its use of such frames of reference as "straw cushion" (*wara-uda*), tangerine and chestnut trees (*shōkōji* and *kuri* respectively), is evidence to indicate that Heian readers by the time of *Ise*'s composition—mostly women of the Court—had already lost contact with the real objects of nature, substituting in their place nature capsulized and miniaturized in the gardens of *shindenzukuri*-style architecture.

The "older brother" is traditionally identified as Yuki-hira (see above, LXXIX), but Mochiyoshi is entirely unknown (he may well be entirely fictional). The job of

Palace Chamberlain (*Kunaikyō*) was the administration of the physical plant of the palace and grounds. The woman is identified in the text as one of the hero's secondary wives.

DAN LXXXVIII: Moon viewing parties, involving wine, music, and the composition of poetry, were traditionally held on the fifteenth day of the eighth month and the thirteenth of the ninth month.

DAN LXXXIX: The hero's poem laments the fact that innocent gods are held responsible for the death of someone who actually died of an unexpressed or secret love. There is no doubt that this is a poetic conceit, but it is admittedly a clever one.

DAN XC: What I have translated as "audience" is *mono-goshi* in the original. The literal meaning of this word is "crossing to within the bounds delimited by the 'curtains of state.'" These curtains were of light brocaded silk, hanging from free-standing wooden frames. Modeled upon the example of T'ang China, they were set up all around the lady's personal dais to secure the utmost privacy.

The characterization of the woman may be applied to the hero as well, depending upon the interpretation we give to the author's comment which ends the episode. Apparently, both the man and woman are so socially mobile that promises of one day tend to lose their significance almost as soon as they are spoken.

DAN XCI: I find this short episode to be quite unique for

this period of Japanese literature. It is extremely rare to find any expression regarding "the conscious passing of time." Ephemerality (*mujōkan*) was generally perceived through concrete objects such as cherry blossoms, a running stream, etc. Here we have a singular example of perception of that spirit through the abstract notion of time. The poem which concludes the episode shows the more normal concept of *mujōkan*; yet, in another context, this *uta* might well be a "death poem."

DAN XCII: The heavy sadness of this poem in the original is achieved by the phrase *tana nashi obune*, "a small boat with no gunnels"; the image is one of a boat so extremely small that it is not noticed as it moves through the tall reeds along the shore.

DAN XCIII: Love between social unequals is a common enough theme in literature, but here it is between high aristocrat and lesser aristocrat. The hero's poem is a rather bold expression, considering the severe strictures of Heian society. The last sentence expresses the author's "surprise" that the severity of "class" distinction was felt "long ago"—apparently aimed at projecting this "modern" poem back into the symbolic era of Narihira.

DAN XCIV: The hero's poem uses the contrast between autumn and spring to stand for the contrast between her new husband and himself. The woman, catching this, is quick to praise the spring (hero); but just as quickly she bemoans both seasons as ephemeral, showing an attitude of defeatism with respect to her own love life.

DAN XCV: For the "curtains," see the notes to XC.

Herdsman Star and the River of Heaven (or the Milky Way) are part of the Tanabata legend discussed in the notes to LXXXII.

The idea of the woman falling in love with the hero after just this one poem is a dramatic fallacy; as the prose indicates from the beginning, the hero had already been endeavoring to achieve this liaison.

DAN XCVI: The Western reader will probably be surprised to find the mention of "boils" in a text whose central aesthetic content is *miyabi* (see above, I). The diary genre of literature flourished during the Heian period with diaries of both fictional and realistic intent. The most outstanding feature of the Japanese representatives of this genre is accurate and explicit truth. The fact that this lady frankly explains her reasons for postponing the visit shows us the probable (if not certain) existence of a truth-oriented diary which was used by the author as a primary source, even though the story is fictionalized. Her poem appears in the *Kokinshū* as one sent to Narihira, which would explain its appearance in the "source" diary.

The historical commentators often identify this woman as Takako in order to explain her brother's action. Her brother would have been anxious to place her in the safety of the Emperor's retinue before the liaison with Narihira could be effected. Nevertheless, I would reject this in order to allow for a more chronological structuring of the *mono-gatari* as a whole. In doing so, I lose a reasonable explanation for the appearance of the brother—but if the hero is to be taken as the center of attention throughout, we need no concrete explanation: this episode rather focuses on the hero's disappointment capsulized at the end.

This disappointment and anger is vented in a vindictive curse. I cannot find any technical explanation of the significance of the manner in which the hero claps his hands; I might suggest, however, that it seems to be a simple reversal of the ordinary hand-clapping used in Shinto worship to request blessings and benefits.

DAN XCVII: The Horikawa Minister was earlier mentioned in the historical interpolation to episode VI (see text). He was Fujiwara no Mototsune (836–91); he was one of Takako's older brothers, his father having been Nagayoshi (or Nagara)—though all of these siblings were made the adoptive children of Yoshifusa (see above, LXXXII). After Yoshifusa's death, Mototsune became Regent (*Sesshō*) and took a new title, that of Civil Dictator (*Kampaku*), bringing Fujiwara rule to a level of complete control. For a description of the birthday celebration, see above, XXIX.

DAN XCVIII: The Grand Prime Minister—usually identified with Fujiwara no Yoshifusa (804–72)—was the highest officer of the civil (as opposed to religious) bureaucracy. The hero's poem to him contains a pun on *kiji*, "pheasant," in the original of the fourth line: *toKI SHI mo wakanu*. This technique of employing the syllables of a poem's subject (*dai*) across word boundaries is called *mono no na*.

DAN XCIX: The "archery contest" referred to would have been held on either the fourth or sixth of the fifth month, the third and fifth days being assigned to contests by the Left Division. In addition to being tests of military prowess, these matches were protection against evil spirits associated with the Tango Festival (see above, LII).

DAN C: The Kōrō Hall is located at the back (west) of the Great Hall (see above, LXV); it housed lesser concubines and their attendants.

Forgetting grass (*wasuregusa*) and passion weed (*shinobugusa*) figure frequently in Japanese *uta*. They were not only confused in actuality—they looked similar—but frequently there was a figurative confusion as well: *shinobugusa* can also mean "hateweed" (see episode I)—which is just the same idea as *wasuregusa*.

DAN CI: For information on Yukihira, see the note to above, LXXIX. Fujiwara no Masachika, a lesser member of this clan, was Auditor of the Left (*Sachūben*) in 874. The Grand Prime Minister (*Ōkiotodo*) referred to was Yoshifusa (see above, LXXXII). If Narihira is to be understood in the background of the hero here, we see a deliberate fictionalization in that he was well known as an outstanding poet.

In the poem there is an intended play between the wistaria (*fuji*) and the Fujiwara clan (see above, LXXX). The interpretation given by the hero in response to a challenge is possible, but his true intention was just that one which spurred the challenge—the Fujiwara were unduly overshadowing all the other clans.

DAN CII: The historical interpolation would have us take this lady as the Priestess of episode LXIX. This is a rather

loose interpretation of the kinship relations between Narihira and Princess Yasuko (Tenshi). She was Koretaka's
sister, who was of Ki stock . . . and so on (see above,
LXXXII).

DAN CIII: Emperor Fukakusa was Emperor Nimmyō
(r. 833–50).

The author's comment on the poem is enigmatic. It is
not much different from many other poems in this work
(and *uta* literature in general) dealing with the ephemerality
of love. It is possible that this is Narihira's personal judg-
ment of his own poem taken directly from the diary, but
this cannot be proved.

DAN CIV: The Kamo Festival, held during the fourth
lunar month, was the most grandiose Court celebration of
the year. It involved almost a month of preparation of
costumes, dances, displays, carriages, horse equipage, foods,
offerings, etc. The Kamo Shrine Virgin (similar in status to
the Ise Virgin) performed a solemn purification rite at the
Kamo River, and the Emperor sent a special emissary to
read the Imperial request for continued blessings for the
nation. The entire aristocratic population of Heian attended
this festival with much pomp and parading—not to mention fighting for the spot most suitable for seeing and being
seen.

The usage of puns in the hero's poem is so intricate that
two entirely different translations are possible. The text
presents the deeper structures; the surface translation might
be as follows:

Weary of the world
you have taken a nun's robes
as I plainly see,
but still you come to Kamo
as I still rely on you.

DAN CV: This rather bold woman sees herself as a wholly free agent who is not automatically obliged to fall in love with the hero whether he is "dying of love" or not. Her use of the standard metaphor of dew and pearls (compare with episode VI) is rather satirical here.

DAN CVI: The use of *chihayaburu* (see above, LXXI) here is translated as "wondrous to behold" in the context of *kamiyo*, "Age of Gods."

The prose preface to this poem in the *Kokinshū* explains that in the palace of the Dowager Empress there was a screen showing the Tatsuta (Dragon Field) River swirling with red autumn leaves.

DAN CVII: It was the job of the Scrivener (*Naiki*) to keep written records of Imperial proclamations, changes in the official ranks and positions of the aristocrats, and Court events—in other words, to be the Court historian. Fujiwara no Toshiyuki was the son of Fujimaro; his was not the main branch of this clan.* As suggested in the notes to

* The main branch, known as the Northern House (*Hokke*), was established by Fubito's son Fusamae; the Southern House (*Nanke*) to which Toshiyuki belonged stemmed from another of Fubito's four sons, Takechimaro.

episode LXIX, his is the name I would like to add to the list of possible "first authors" of *Ise-monogatari* (see the notes to LXIII for a working definition of *author*).

As a member of a politically unimportant branch of the Fujiwara clan, Toshiyuki could have shared the sentiments of the other great clans while simultaneously escaping any direct pressures on his own family. As Ki no Aritsune's nephew and son-in-law, he would be drawn even closer to outright sympathy for the Ki and the Arihara clans. As Narihira's brother-in-law, he would have had access to the "source diary."

Toshiyuki had reason, opportunity, and the ability to write the first version of *Ise-monogatari*. What clue is there in the work, however, to even tentatively admit my selection of him? Of all the historical figures who appear in the tales there are only two who are presented in a bad light; they are Minamoto no Itaru and Fujiwara no Toshiyuki. In the notes to XXXIX I have explained the case of Itaru and the emendation of the picture made in the historical interpolation. This leaves Toshiyuki. The caricature of him which this episode presents is of a man so inept and ignorant in the ideals of *miyabi* and *irogonomi* that he must be more than a fictional foil for the hero. In short, I believe this caricature to be a self-degrading portrait of the author. I make this suggestion not in an attempt to contribute directly to the problem of the authorship of *Ise-monogatari*, but indirectly in endeavoring to explain the special characterization of Toshiyuki in this episode.

DAN CVIII: The woman's poem is a jumble of stock images—wind, whitecaps, crags, drenched sleeves, sea foam. This shows that she is rather limited in her responses to social situations. The hero's reply presents a rather comical image. The verb *naku,* besides meaning "to cry tears," can also mean, in the frog's case, "to croak"; the word "cry" is used in order to accommodate both meanings.

DAN CIX: The tenor of this episode seems very close to XVI; for this reason, I have translated *hito* as "wife" rather than as "mistress, someone dear" or just "a woman."

DAN CX: The hero's poem is definitely comical in intent. He suggests that, if his soul should escape his body and visit her a second time (see above, LIV), she should ward it off with "magic" (*tamamusubi*), literally "incantations." In addition to meaning "magic," *tamamusubi* can mean "strung beads," an allusive reference, perhaps, to the Buddhist rosary (*juzudama*).

DAN CXI: The untying of the trouser cord is symbolic of the active side of a love affair; the hero's sensuality is less prominent in the original than in the idiom of my translation. The lack of the normal circumlocutions expected in the Japanese, however, suggested to me the more direct expression.

DAN CXII: This episode demonstrates the nature of the technical difficulties which the translator must solve during the process of his work. In the manuscript, a photocopy of which has been used throughout as the primary text, the entire prose segment of this episode is written in a very small hand on the left edge of a page (verso, 80), making it the twelfth line on that page. This is uncommon as most of the pages have either nine or ten lines of text. The small size of the script is enough to tempt the translator into suggesting that the "original" form of this episode had no prose. This prose cannot be an interpolation from the text known as the *Takeda-bon,* from which other collations are added in the margins and to the right of the pertinent word, because there is an even smaller notation of this type to the right of *chigireru,* "had promised," showing a variant of *chigirikeru,* a simpler past tense.

Nevertheless, I cannot reconcile the calligraphy with any logical event in the history of this text (generally known as the Tempuku). I can understand that Sanjōnishi Sanetaka (1455–1537) faithfully copied this sentence in smaller script as he may have found it in the original copy by Fujiwara no Sadaie (or Teika, 1162–1241), but I find it odd that he would not somehow either readjust the entire page or merely transpose this line to the next page (reverse, 80). Assuming that he was reproducing the text exactly page for page as Teika had, it does nothing to explain why Teika himself should have found it so necessary to cram this line onto this particular page. If we look to the end of the manuscript for some explanation we are denied it, because there are only six lines on the last page of text. (More surprisingly, the poem in CXXV takes three lines, in contradistinction to any of the other poems in the tales, which take only two lines.) Thus, we are left right where we started.

I would suggest that the materials which became the basis for these Tempuku manuscripts (so called from the colophon dated in the second year of the Tempuku era,

1234) had no prose preceding this poem and that the prose was collated from some other textual family with which Teika was familiar. I might tentatively propose that this poem was a segment of the preceding episode as its sentiment closely resembles the general tone of that tale. This is possible in that the poem of CII is no more than a rewriting of no. 1246 in the *Manyōshū*. I have, nevertheless, translated the prose as a fully instated part of the text in order to maintain the structural integrity of this episode in the light of the format of the whole. This would appear to be the central reasoning used by Teika as well when he interpolated this prose passage into the Tempuku text.

DAN CXIII: That the man was living alone (*yamome*) could indicate either that he had divorced his wife or that she had died. The tone of the poem seems to favor the former interpretation.

DAN CXIV: Emperor Ninna (r. 884–87) made his trip to Serikawa in 887. This episode is clearly extrahistorical with respect to Narihira.

The crane in the poem is the traditional East Asian symbol of longevity.

DAN CXV: The first line of the poem, *okinoite*, is an untranslatable pun on the place name in the text, Okinoite; *oki* means "embers," and *ite* translates in the sense of "being placed on the body."

DAN CXVI: If we look at the *ruika* (see above, XXXV) in the *Manyōshū*, no. 2753, the "huts' thatch eaves" (*hama-*

bisashi) could be taken as *hamahisaki*, "a shore-oak." The word in the *Ise-monogatari* is, by its uniqueness, either a miscopying or a coining.

DAN CXVII: The Shinto deity mentioned here was a trinity of marine protectors—Uwatsutsuno-onomikoto, Nakatsutsuno-onomikoto, and Sokotsutsuno-onomikoto; protectors at the surface, midpoint, and bottom of the seas. The verb *gegyō-suru* means to take on sentient form or to "manifest" oneself; in this case we are to suppose that the manifestation of the god was in the form of one of the pine trees.

DAN CXVIII: The first part of this poem seems to have clear sexual overtones if we read it in the context of a folk poem; here, however, we see the second half carrying the fuller meaning which would obviate those overtones.

DAN CXIX: The severity of the woman's distress gives us a good idea of the emotion our fictional hero could be responsible for. We should not, however, ever see him as an unfeeling Byronic Don Juan.

DAN CXX: The insulting tone of the poem is interestingly achieved in a one-to-one correspondence between *nabe* and "stewpots." This tone is, of course, connected to the *hinabi* of the provinces (see above, XIV).

DAN CXXI: The Plum Blossom Apartments (*Umetsubo*) was a ladies' residence in the Imperial Palace.

The image of the nightingale (*uguisu*) sewing a rain hat of plum blossoms comes from a folk poem in the *saibara* form where these blossoms are sewn with the strings of the weeping willow. The *saibara* form—of which we have only some sixty examples—was prevalent in the provinces immediately surrounding the capital during the late Nara and early Heian periods.

DAN CXXII: In the poem, the image of water slipping through the hands is parallel to pouring meaningless promises into a cup with no bottom.

DAN CXXIII: This woman is interesting because, through her *miyabi* (see above, I), she is able to recapture the hero's affections after he has become bored with their affair and her provincial setting.

DAN CXXIV: From the point of the overall structure of the tales, I consider this episode to be extremely important. Here the hero is totally isolated, as if he were about to sum up his entire life (which he is). The poignancy of this situation is that the poet finds his poetic isolation within the very society which he has come to symbolize. Perhaps the poet is sincere in his wish that no soul try to comprehend the totality of any other soul—I find this a fitting sentiment for so sensitive a poet. The interlude of introspective quietude which this episode creates shows, perhaps more than any other structural feature in the *Ise-monogatari*, the existence of some fictional and aesthetic superstructure existing in the mind of the creator(s) of this work.

DAN CXXV: The hero is aware, classically, that he is about to die; but this does not interfere in any way with the beauty of his "death poem."

In the poem itself we find the idea that the hero is neither ready nor willing to die "today." Since he could not bear the thought "yesterday" or "today," we may suppose that the poem is written during an unstated "tonight." All of this reluctance and hesitation, the playing with temporal relations, however, is mere *style* dictated by his *miyabi* and *irogonomi*. The great man, the great poet, the great lover— here, even on his deathbed, he is simply following the canons of poetic taste—a most elegant end to his symbolic life within these tales.

NOTES ON THE ILLUSTRATIONS

FIG. 1 (*Dan I*): The hero is shown speaking with one of the ladies-in-waiting to the two sisters. The sisters are shown facing us along with another of their retinue. The two deer shown in the left foreground are associated with the area around Nara, here specifically the village of Kasuga.

FIG. 2 (*Dan IV*): The hero is shown seated in the now deserted room where he had hoped to meet his love the previous year. He is staring blankly at the plum blossoms in the left foreground as the moon begins to set.

FIG. 3 (*Dan VI*): The hero is shown carrying the princess with whom he has absconded. They have just passed the Akuta River which is depicted in such fashion as to suggest the stream in Mishima near Osaka rather than the artificial stream of the same name in the Imperial Palace grounds as suggested by the editorial interpolation.

FIG. 4 (*Dan IX*): We are shown four or five of the eight bridges at Yatsuhashi in this picture. The hero sits facing us, and his two companions, similarly dressed, sit with him at the edge of the marsh. The *kakitsubata* flags are shown in three clumps. The dried rice provisions are on trays shown before the hero and the companion on the right.

FIG. 5 (*Dan XII*):   Two fire-bearing officials and a third with readied bow are shown about to fire the Musashi field where the hero and his love are shown hiding in the tall grasses, center left. The facial portraiture of the officials is clearly reminiscent of the style used to depict the commoners in the Ban Dainagon Scrolls of the Kamakura period.

FIG. 6 (*Dan XVIII*):   The lady of this episode is shown seated in her room, having sent one of her ladies to the hero bearing a spray of fading chrysanthemums to test his love.

FIG. 7 (*Dan XXIII*):   The children are shown at the well, the girl to the left, the boy to the right. The architecture of the house in the background suggests the less than aristocratic status of the characters.

FIG. 8 (*Dan XLV*):   The hero sits watching the fireflies at night while he mourns for the dead woman who failed to express her love for him. Irises are shown blooming in the stream running through the garden.

FIG. 9 (*Dan L*):   The woman of this episode is shown at the bank of a river, beneath a pine tree, trying to write on the surface of the water, thus illustrating the poem.

FIG. 10 (*Dan LXIII*):   The "old" lady, commonly known

as *tsukumogami* (wizened hair), is spying on the hero who had taken pity at her plight and given her a night of love. In contrast with the rural architecture of the house in the first episode, where the fence is of woven bamboo, here the fence is of green bamboo and the screens are more elegantly constructed.

FIG. 11 (*Dan LXIX*): The hero sits looking out toward the hall and beyond that the garden. The moon indicates the hour of night. The Shrine Priestess stands hesitantly in the corridor while her handmaiden precedes her into the room. The softness and balance of the scene are enhanced by the lighted lampstand next to the man's pillow.

FIG. 12 (*Dan LXXVIII*): Prince Yamashina and the hero are shown looking at the watercourses in the Prince's garden. General of the Right Tsuneyuki and his attendant sit to their left. The architecture of the roof in the left foreground, as well as the Prince's tonsure and robes, give the feeling of a Buddhist retreat.

FIG. 13 (*Dan LXXXVII*): The hero and his brother, both Captains in the Palace Guard, look at the Nunobiki Falls with one other lesser member of their group. The hero seems to be the man in the middle facing us, while the man reciting is his brother.

FIG. 14 (*Dan XCV*): The hero has entreated one of the Empress's attendants to meet him without the screen of state between them. She is shown just peeping out from one side as he stands impatiently on the veranda.

FIG. 15 (*Dan CXIX*): The woman of this episode is shown seated within her screens of state crying as she looks at the things the hero has left behind as mementos of his relationship with her. Shown are a *koto*, his Court robe and headgear. Her attendant sits in the left foreground. The heavy lines of the pine tree suggest a solemn finality which deepens the sadness of this scene.

FIG. 16 (*Dan CXXV*): The hero is shown in his last moments, lying behind his screens and attended by a young retainer. Pathos is achieved by the combination of his death with the hint of a flourishing setting of nature.

APPENDICES

KEY:

W1   West First
W2   West Second
W3   West Third
W4   West Fourth
W5   West Fifth
W6   West Sixth
W7   West Seventh
W8   West Eighth
W9   West Ninth

10 West Capital Avenue
11 West Palace Avenue
12 Suzaku Boulevard
13 Mibu Street East
14 East Palace Avenue
15 Horikawa Street
16 West Tōin Avenue
17 Muromachi Street
18 East Tōin Avenue
19 Madenokōji
20 East Capital Avenue

E1   East First
     (a) Tsuchimikado Street
     (b) Konoe Street
     (c) Nakamikado Street
     (d) Ōimikado Street
E2   East Second
E3   East Third
E4   East Fourth
E5   East Fifth
E6   East Sixth
E7   East Seventh
E8   East Eighth
E9   East Ninth

1   Suzaku Gate
2   Rajō Gate
3   East Fifth Palace

4   Right Division Stables
5   Nijō Palace
6   East Second Palace

STREET PLAN OF THE HEIAN CAPITAL

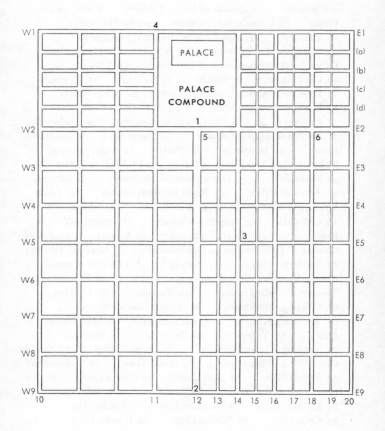

KEY:

1 Palace   2 Eight Bureaus' Office   3 Great Banquet Hall
4 Bureau of Ceremony   5 Bureau of People's Affairs
6 Chancery   7 Bureau of Internal Affairs   8 Divination
Office   9 Chamberlain's Office   10 Nobles' Office
11 Granary   12 Bureau of the Imperial Household
13 Sai-in   14 Shūsuishi   15 Shoin   16 Court Music
Office   17 Department of Worship   18 Tōin
19 Cookhouse   20 Pantry   21 Saigain   22 Tōgain
23 Page Boys' Office   24 Library   25 South Room
26 Foreign Records Office   27 Left Division Guards
28 Cadets   29 Left Division Inner Guards   30 Nashimoto
31 Bureau of Military Affairs   32 Danjōdai   33 Bureau of
Justice   34 Bureau of Civil Affairs   35 Right Division
Stables   36 Left Division Stables   37 Mediate Office
38 Wellhouse   39 Department of Medicine   40 Brewery
41 Artisans' Office   42 Right Division Guards   43 Right
Division Inner Guards   44 Butokuden   45 Shingon-in
46 Chūwain   47 Imperial Kitchen   48 Attendants'
Residence   49 Maids' Residence   50 Library   51 Poetry
Office   52 Maintenance Department   53 Imperial Treasury
54 Uniforms Office   55 Nan-in   56 Office of Imperial
Family Records   57 Seamstresses' Office   58 Bureau of the
Treasury   59 Treasury   60 Treasury   61 Chōden
62 Offerings Storehouse   63 Central Guard House
64 Women's School   65 Tea Garden   66 Maintenance
Office   67 Treasury   68 Treasury   69 Treasury
70 Treasury   71 Armory   72 Lacquer Shop   73 Suzaku
Gate   74 Bifuku Gate   75 Ikuhō Gate   76 Taiken Gate
77 Yōmei Gate   78 Jōtō Gate   79 Datchi Gate   80 Ikan
Gate   81 Anki Gate   82 Jōsai Gate   83 Inbu Gate
84 Shōheki Gate   85 Danten Gate   86 Kōka Gate
87 Ōten Gate   88 Shōkei Gate   89 Buraku Gate
90 Furō Gate   91 Kenrei Gate

APPENDIX II

Plan of the Palace Compound

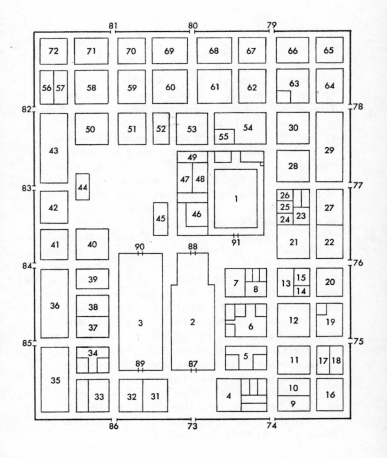

KEY:

1 Shishinden   2 Great August Dais   3 Jijūden
4 Jōkyōden   5 Seiryōden   6 Kōrōden   7 Wistaria
Apartments (Hikyōsha)   8 Plum Blossom Apartments
(Gyōkasha)   9 Raimei Apartments (Shihōsha)   10 Kokiden
11 Tōkaden   12 Jōneiden   13 Jōganden   14 Reikeiden
15 Sen-yōden   16 Pear Blossom Apartments (Shōyōsha)
17 Northern Wing   18 Pawlonia Wood Apartments
(Shigeisha)   19 Northern Wing   20 Dragon Barrack
21 Library   22 Ryōkiden   23 Palace Sanctuary(Ummeiden)
24 Palanquin Shed   25 Great Storehouse (Giyōden)
26 Shunkyōden   27 Shukiden   28 Breezeway
29 Cherry Tree of the Left   30 Mandarin Orange Tree of the
Right   31 Armory   32 Bureau of Legations (Kyōshoden)
33 Anfukuden   34 Treasury   35 Supplies   36 Supplies
37 Repair Shop   38 Shōmei Gate   39 Chōraku Gate
40 Ensei Gate   41 Sen-yō Gate   42 Kayō Gate   43 Anki
Gate   44 Genki Gate   45 Kian Gate   46 Yūgi Gate
47 Immei Gate   48 Butoku Gate   49 Eian Gate
50 Gekka Gate   51 Nikka Gate   52 Orchid Grove
53 Katsura Grove   54 Flower Grove   55 Water House
56 Kenrei Gate   57 Shunka Gate   58 Kenshun Gate
59 Sakuhei Gate   60 Shikiken Gate   61 Gishū Gate
62 Kyōjō Gate   63 Shumei Gate   64 Ritual Hall
65 West Wing   66 East Wing   67 North Wing
68 Middle Gate   69 West Gate   70 East Gate
71 Carpentry   72 Imperial Kitchen   73 Attendants'
Residence   74 Maids' Residence

APPENDIX III

PLAN OF THE IMPERIAL PALACE

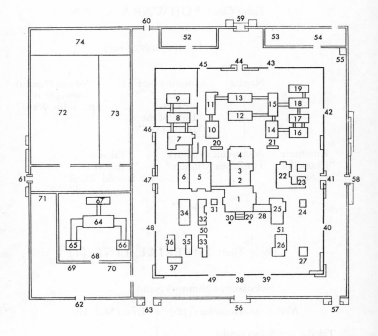

APPENDIX IV

Genealogical Relationships

Table One: FUJIWARA CLAN

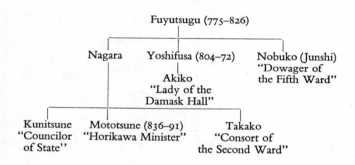

Table Two: IMPERIAL LINE (1)

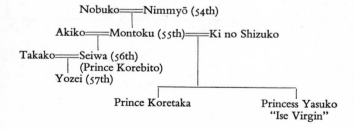

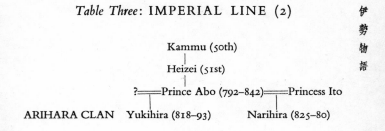

Table Three: IMPERIAL LINE (2)

Kammu (50th)
|
Heizei (51st)
|
?══Prince Abo (792–842)══Princess Ito
| |
ARIHARA CLAN   Yukihira (818–93)   Narihira (825–80)

伊
勢
物
語

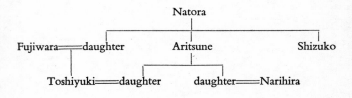

Table Four: KI CLAN

Natora
|
Fujiwara══daughter   Aritsune   Shizuko
| |
Toshiyuki══daughter   daughter══Narihira

SELECTED AND ANNOTATED
BIBLIOGRAPHY

As stated in the Introduction, this volume is a literary translation and not a scholarly work. Naturally, much scholarship has gone into the production of this book, but the Western reader could gain nothing from a full bibliographical listing of the several hundred Japanese publications from which I have benefited greatly. For the purposes of documentation, however, I note the following four major works in Japanese.

Ikeda, Kikan. *Ise-monogatari ni tsukite no kenkyū* [Studies of *Tales of Ise*]. 3 vols. Tokyo: Ōokayama Shobō, Shōwa 8–9 (1933–34).

    To date this work remains the most comprehensive study of *Tales of Ise*. In addition to extended analysis of the major problems of authorship, date of composition, transmission, relationships of textual families and textual variations, Dr. Ikeda's work includes major scholarly contributions by scholars of the caliber of Ōtsu Yūichi and Fukui Teisuke. The only area of research which has been neglected is that which deals with aesthetics and the overall structure of the *monogatari*. Unfortunately, no such work has appeared or is likely to appear from those scholars in Japan who have carried on Dr. Ikeda's work since his death in 1956.

Ikeda, Kikan. *Ise-monogatari Seikō* [*Tales of Ise*—a Reader's Edition]. Tokyo: Gakutei-sha, Shōwa 30 (1955).

This small work presents the *monogatari* in full with an introductory essay of great value to the student which has been provided by Dr. Fukui Teisuke. In presenting each episode with notes, commentary, and translation into modern Japanese, Dr. Ikeda has provided a highly valuable edition of this work for the beginning student.

Ōtsu, Yūichi, and Tsukishima, Yutaka, eds. and annotators. *Ise-monogatari* [*Tales of Ise*]. Included in Vol. IX of *Nihon Koten Bungaku Taikei* [Grand Compendium of Classical Japanese Literature], gen'l. eds. Takagi, Ichinosuke *et al.* Tokyo: Iwanami Shoten, Shōwa 32 (1957).

This edition is the standard text for *Tales of Ise*. The series in which it is included is also the most generally available collection of classical Japanese literature. The scholarship of Drs. Ōtsu and Tsukishima, while limited by the general nature of its presentation within a mammoth series, is almost faultless.

Suzuki, Tomotarō, ed. and annotator. *Gakushūin Daigaku Zōhon Ise-monogatari* [The *Tales of Ise* Manuscript in the Collection of Gakushūin University]. Tokyo: Musashino Shoin, Shōwa 38 (1963).

This is a photographic reproduction of the oldest and most reliable manuscript of *Tales of Ise*. Throughout the work of producing my translation, this book has been the sole source for the text. Consequently, I have deleted words collated from texts of the "Takeda" line commonly found in the standard editions listed above.

This manuscript, attributed to Fujiwara Teika, was long in the possession of the descendants of Sanjōnishi Sanetaka. Preserved in its black lacquer box, the manuscript measures 16.33 cm. by 16.17 cm.; there are in all ninety-two leaves, ninety of which bear writing. The first and last leaves serve as covers, the former bearing the title *Ise-monogatari* in the center. The text begins on the reverse of leaf two and ends with six lines on the reverse of leaf eighty-five. The remaining leaves contain brief histories of relevant historical figures, explanations of difficult terms, and the colophons of the Tempuku and Takeda traditions.

Tales of Ise has twice before this been presented in full English translation. For the comparatist and those interested in different types of translation, the citations follow.

McCullough, Helen Craig. *Tales of Ise: Lyrical Episodes from Tenth-Century Japan.* Stanford: Stanford U.Pr., 1968.

Vos, Frits. *A Study of the Ise-Monogatari with the text according to the Den-Teika-Hippon and an annotated translation* (2 vols.). The Hague: Mouton & Co., 1957.

> Dr. Vos presents a thoroughly detailed study of *Ise* which seems heavily indebted to Dr. Ikeda's three-volume work. His translation in no way attempts to present the *monogatari* as literature. Nevertheless, his detailed notes dealing primarily with grammar and etymology are a valuable source of explication through example for the Western student of classical Japanese. Mrs. McCullough's translation attempts to straddle the fence between the scholarly and the artistic. The result is one which might be expected—neither area is adequately treated.

The following six works may be used by the Western reader to gain a general familiarity with the history, techniques, and cultural heritage of classical Japanese literature. While some of these books deal too superficially with their contents, they are the best and most easily obtainable of the contributions presently available in the field.

Bownas, Geoffrey and Thwaite, Anthony. *The Penguin Book of Japanese Verse.* Baltimore: Penguin Books Ltd., 1964.

> This small anthology may be highly recommended, not only

for the general content and quality of translation but also for an extremely concise and well-thought-out introduction.

Keene, Donald. *Japanese Literature: An Introduction for Western Readers.* New York: Grove Press, 1955.

A short introductory work, this book has many faults of which Dr. Keene is himself aware, and should be used with discretion. I particularly take exception to the ideas that *Tales of Ise* has no unifying concept, that it is comparable to *La Vita Nuova,* and that Narihira is the hero of many episodes.

Miner, Earl. *An Introduction to Japanese Court Poetry.* Stanford: Stanford U. Pr., *1968.*

This volume, a paperback (and for that reason alone preferable), is generally a shorter version of the work done in collaboration with R. H. Brower in 1961. While the translations nowhere attain the level of poetry found in the originals, the chapters on form, prosody, convention, and themes are useful to the student of the technical aspects of Japanese poetry.

Morris, Ivan. *The World of the Shining Prince: Court Life in Ancient Japan.* New York: Alfred A. Knopf, 1964.

Dr. Morris's work is essential to the understanding of the cultural milieu which produced the major works *Tales of Ise* and *The Tale of Genji.* While this book is concerned only with the latter, almost all of the cultural information is applicable to the earlier work—though not in so categorical a manner. Of all the books available to the Western reader, this one volume will be the most valuable for an understanding of the whole of classical Japanese literature.

Waley, Arthur. *Japanese Poetry: The "Uta."* London: Perry Lund, Humphries & Co. Ltd., 1956. (First edition: The Clarendon Press, 1919.)

Western readers interested in Japanese literature have no doubt come to realize that any bibliography on a part of that field will include at least one work by this giant to whom all within the field are so greatly indebted. This volume of *uta* poetry is now available in a paperback edition. While it is of no major consequence, it may serve as an excellent entrance into the literature of this form for those wholly unfamiliar with the Japanese language.

Waley, Arthur. *The Tale of Genji*. The Modern Library. New York: Random House, 1960.

This edition, because of its general use and availability, is listed in preference to the original two volumes issued in 1935 by Houghton Mifflin.

While *Tales of Ise* cannot be considered "better" than this work, it should not be considered "less." Moreover, the later *monogatari* is much in debt to the one presented in this volume. Further, *Tales of Ise* has historically had a far greater impact on Japanese literature than this work which signals the end of "Court" literature. If there are readers of this volume who have not yet experienced Dr. Waley's *Genji*, they would do well to read it along with Morris's work. In spite of the many criticisms leveled at this translation—and no matter how valid or applicable these be—this is the only translation we have. That fact should by no means be a deterrent, for there was a time when there was but one English version of Homer.